WOODSTOCK'S
INFAMOUS
MURDER TRIAL

WOODSTOCK'S INFAMOUS MURDER TRIAL

EARLY RACIAL INJUSTICE
IN UPSTATE NEW YORK

RICHARD HEPPNER

THE
History
PRESS

Published by The History Press
Charleston, SC
www.historypress.com

Copyright © 2020 by Richard Heppner
All rights reserved

Front cover: courtesy of the Historical Society of Woodstock Archives.
Back cover: courtesy of the Friends of Historic Kingston; *inset*: courtesy of the Ulster County Clerk's Office.

First published 2020
Manufactured in the United States

ISBN 9781467144766

Library of Congress Control Number: 2019951252

Notice: The information in this book is true and complete to the best of our knowledge. It is offered without guarantee on the part of the author or The History Press. The author and The History Press disclaim all liability in connection with the use of this book.

All rights reserved. No part of this book may be reproduced or transmitted in any form whatsoever without prior written permission from the publisher except in the case of brief quotations embodied in critical articles and reviews.

To all Woodstockers who work to ensure that "justice for all" actually means something.

CONTENTS

Acknowledgements	9
Introduction	11
1. The Headlines	15
2. Woodstock, 1905	17
3. December 5 and 6, 1905	25
4. The Chase	33
5. Augustus H. Van Buren	38
6. Interlude: The Trial Approaches	49
7. Jury Selection	52
8. Testimony	57
9. Van Gaasbeek Takes the Stand	69
10. Summations and Verdict	74
11. Aftermath	77
12. Faint Hope	80
13. The Final Battle	86
14. The Journey Ends	104
15. Moving On	106
Afterword: The Road We Have Traveled	115
Bibliography	123
About the Author	125

ACKNOWLEDGEMENTS

The pursuit of local history and the discoveries that can be found along the way would not be possible without the efforts of so many. With thanks to the Historical Society of Woodstock; the *Woodstock Times* and Brian Hollander; the Kingston Library and its microfilm collection; Hudson River Valley Heritage and the Southeastern New York Library Resources Council for their continued digitization efforts; the Friends of Historic Kingston; and the Ulster County Clerk's Office, Nina Postupack, County Clerk for their generous assistance. Individually, thanks also to Taylor Bruck, Paul O'Neill, Jane Kellar, Peter Roberts, Ed Sanders and Deborah Heppner for their assistance.

INTRODUCTION

At its core, this is a story about a murder that took place in Woodstock, New York, in 1905. The accused was a black man named Cornell Van Gaasbeek. The victim was a young white man named Oscar Harrison. By extension, it is also about the legal proceedings that surrounded Van Gaasbeek's case for almost three years. This is also a story that goes beyond the courtroom, however. It is about the many once unconnected lives of individuals drawn together during those years and the public stage they shared.

It is also a story about context. Five years into the twentieth century—and only forty years removed from the Civil War—Woodstock and Ulster County had only begun to emerge from a decidedly rural, somewhat isolated existence into a new world of electrification, tourism and cultural change. It was a change that came slowly and one in which changing racial attitudes came even slower.

The plight of Cornell Van Gaasbeek and the justice system he encountered in 1905 was not a story this author, frankly, went looking for. Rather, it is one I stumbled on while researching a different topic in local newspapers. Eventually, that initial encounter with Van Gaasbeek's case led to a two-part essay for the *Woodstock Times*. Thinking the story was behind me, I moved on. At least that was the intent. As time passed, however, something kept pulling me back across the years, across more than a century of changing attitudes, beliefs and perceptions. History, for some, may be about major events strung together over time. History, to me, is also about the individual lives and stories that make up the intertwining threads of the overall tapestry. Such is the reason I returned to the story of Cornell Van Gaasbeek, a black man accused of murder in a rural, northern town populated almost exclusively by white people.

Van Gaasbeek's story also includes his lawyer, Augustus H. Van Buren. A well-to-do politician and lawyer of impeccable Ulster County lineage, Augustus Van Buren may have been the least likely person to rise as the champion of Van Gaasbeek's cause. And yet, there he was in newspaper article after newspaper article, overseeing a defense that he knew was without guarantee in a world where a black man of no financial means faced a system that continued to prop up the era of Jim Crow. In some respects, while the fight Van Buren took on was a fight that, today, we might equate with Harper Lee's fictional *To Kill a Mockingbird*, the reality of young Harrison's death and the obstacles that would confront Van Buren's efforts to secure justice for Van Gaasbeek were, at the time, burdens that fell heavily on Van Buren's shoulders.

A further word about context: Throughout the following pages, as the original transcripts have long since passed into history, the story that is presented relies heavily on reporting from the *Kingston Daily Freeman* and other sources beginning in 1905. As a result, the reader must consider the context of published reports using the word *Negro* and other racial references not in common use today. Such usage, while long out of publishing favor, was, in both local and national newspapers, common for the day. That said, what was also common was the sense of hierarchy and class differences between races that often comes across in both the testimony and reporting from the trial. Viewed from the perspective of today's acceptance of diversity and inclusiveness, such attitudes are, at times, difficult to consider. This, however, is the way we were, and while we are often not shy at approaching past racial injustices on a national level, we should not be shy when honestly approaching our past locally. Negative attitudes surrounding race have existed in all chapters of our national story; that they also existed on a local level should come as no surprise.

With the above noted, the story that follows is not only about race and justice. It is also a story of a small town emerging into the twentieth century. Wedged between what had been and what was on the horizon, Woodstock—and Ulster County—was being pulled into recognizing that change was coming, despite how much a number of local citizens desired to hold on to the past. The old ways of farming, tanning and bluestone quarrying were being supplanted by the arrival of artists and seasonal

INTRODUCTION

visitors as both embraced the physical beauty of the surrounding landscape. Having been isolated at the entrance to the Catskill Mountains for so many years, notice and attention from outsiders had not been actively sought. That, however, was changing.

Both Woodstock and Ulster County in 1905 were distinctly conservative in their politics and in the individuals chosen to administer justice. One of the few exceptions to that rule was Augustus Van Buren, a prime mover in the local Democratic Party and one who proudly wore the label of "reformer." The conservative nature of life in Ulster County at the time would present Van Gaasbeek's attorney with dual challenges as his defense moved forward. Not only would the legal battle before him find Van Buren struggling to contest the evidence against Van Gaasbeek, but it would also call on him to confront attitudes and beliefs that had been firmly set in the hearts and minds of potential jurors, the trial's principle witnesses, his legal opposition, a skeptical public and, at times, a questioning press. In many respects, as the machinery of early twentieth-century justice would grind away in the county courthouse in Kingston, the lines drawn were not just about guilt or innocence but also a reflection on ideological differences spawned by changing times.

As we study and reflect on our past, it is only human, as previously noted, to be drawn to the major events, accomplishments and individuals that have shaped us as a people. As a result, the lives of everyday people

The village of Woodstock at the base of Overlook Mountain. *Courtesy of Historical Society of Woodstock Archives.*

Introduction

and the road they have traveled are readily moved to the margins. But, as we view the grand scope of our history, the careful observer will come to realize that the pages that fully tell our story are mostly filled by a continuum of interconnecting lives—lives and actions that have formed the bricks and mortar of a past on which the present has been constructed. Such lives and events, as historian Howard Zinn has offered, "emphasize new possibilities by disclosing those hidden episodes of the past when, even if in brief flashes, people showed their ability to resist, to join together [and] occasionally to win."

The story that follows, however small the space it occupies on the timeline of our history, is one of those "brief flashes" that Zinn refers to, a point in time when resistance and belief battled to counter the prevailing forces of the day.

1
THE HEADLINES

Foul Murder Near Woodstock
Oscar Harrison, Aged 23, the Victim of the Crime
His Dead Body Found in the House of a Colored Man Named Cornell
Van Gaasbeek, Who Is Missing—Search Being Made for Him
District Attorney Notified

Oscar Harrison, 23 years old, and a son of John H. Harrison, superintendent of reservoir No.1 of Kingston water works, was found brutally murdered this morning in the house of a colored man named Cornell Van Gaasbeek, about two miles from the village of Woodstock. His head was battered in, and he had been dead for some time when the body was found.

Van Gaasbeek and Harrison were seen together early this morning but when the body was discovered the colored man was no where to be found. It is thought that he disappeared from the vicinity after committing the crime.

So read the news on page five of the *Kingston Daily Freeman* on the evening of December 5, 1905. While most Woodstock readers would not see the article until the next day, word had already begun to spread through the small town as the sun crossed past the noon hour. Life in 1905 may have moved slowly for the residents at the base of Overlook Mountain, but with the crime of murder in the air and a murderer in their midst, tongues would speak of nothing else. And, as the headline in the *Kingston Daily Leader*

BRUTALLY MURDERED

Oscar Harrison Found With His Head Battered In.

COLORED FELLOW SUSPECTED

Headline as it appeared in the *Kingston Daily Leader*. Retrieved from microfilm printout. The Kingston Library.

the following day would further offer, fingers were already pointing in the direction of the man the local papers had clearly implicated in the horrific act, Cornell Van Gaasbeek.

> *Brutally Murdered*
> *Oscar Harrison Found with His Head Battered In*
> *Color Fellow Suspected*
>
> *Cornell Van Gaasbeek, who is missing and at whose home in Woodstock the body of Harrison was found, believed guilty of the crime—Sheriff Webster's deputies and posses searching for the murderer.*

2
WOODSTOCK, 1905

Small-town life has long been a part of American lore. From Thornton Wilder's Grover's Corners to Garrison Keillor's Lake Wobegon, the depiction of small-town, rural America invokes an element of nostalgia and an image of a simpler, easier way of life. Idyllic, if you will, a place where a sense of belonging is known, where character is nurtured and shaped and where families and neighbors take care of each other.

Then again, in a town where everyone knows your name, there is also a good chance that everyone also knows your "business," or at least think they do. In short, small towns can have a darker side to them. They can easily thrive on gossip. Their citizens can quickly turn suspicious, engage in ostracism, foster bigotry and, when trouble comes calling, direct blame at those they deem "different" or "lesser" than themselves.

Such was the Woodstock that Cornell Van Gaasbeek found in 1905.

As a black man living in a dilapidated structure in the Woodstock hamlet of Zena near the corners of Sawkill and Zena Roads, Van Gaasbeek knew his position in the community was not a lofty one. That position was connected to an equally rundown house next door, where his three nephews and their father—one of whom shared his bed with a white woman—lived. The Conine family—brothers George, Arthur and Albert along with their father Hiram and Emma Smith—had also been the object of gossip and head shaking about town. Only recently, one press report had labeled Van Gaasbeek and the Conine family as Woodstock's "bad lot."

Described as a well-known "character," Van Gaasbeek had moved from Kingston to occupy a small house in Zena, depicted in the *Kingston Daily Freeman* as "not presenting an inviting appearance either inside or out." Similarly, his physical description as reported in the press did little to elevate his stature in the eyes of the reading public. Believed, erroneously at first, to be about forty-five years old, Van Gaasbeek was described as a stout man standing approximately five feet, eight inches tall who walked "with a lope and shuffles his feet." Noting that he was someone who worked only odd jobs about town, the paper concluded, "He is considered lazy by those who knew him."

Similarly, when the *Kingston Daily Leader* reached its readers on the day following the discovery of Oscar Harrison's body, the story that fell beneath the "Brutally Murdered" headline described Van Gaasbeek as having always been "of a lazy disposition" and a "shiftless fellow."

In addition to the contextual racism of the era, the "bad lot" characterization that surrounded both Van Gaasbeek and the Conines seems to have also stemmed from suspicions around Woodstock that the family was responsible for a recent wave of chicken thefts reported in town, including the disappearance of multiple birds from the Norman Lasher family. And, while we may not equate the stealing of chickens with that of horse theft in the old west, stealing home-raised chickens in a rural town was considered a major offense, even a felony in some instances. Long before Woodstockers could walk into a local market and purchase ready-to-go poultry, chickens and eggs were not only a major component of local diets but also a source of income for many. To steal a chicken in early twentieth-century Woodstock was, literally, to steal food off a family's table and money from their pockets. So seriously was such theft viewed that two local men, convicted on charges of stealing chickens, had been sentenced to serve a prison term in New York's Dannemora Prison.

Woodstock in 1905, despite the recent influx of artists who had arrived in town with the founding of Ralph Whitehead's Byrdcliffe art colony, was a decidedly rural and conservative town. While electricity and phone service had arrived for a few, horse-drawn wagons remained the primary source of transportation over the town's unpaved roads. Life not only moved slowly, but also, for the most part, Woodstock "news" that found its way into local papers often ranged from who visited whom on a given Sunday to what was being served at the next church dinner.

Though the town wouldn't realize it for a number of years, probably the most important event that would occur in 1905 was the result of a dispute

The center of Woodstock as it appeared in the early years of the twentieth century. *Courtesy of Historical Society of Woodstock Archives.*

between Ralph Whitehead and his associate, Hervey White. At odds with Whitehead regarding his oversight of the Byrdcliffe art colony, White would leave Byrdcliffe and, along with Fritz van der Loo, purchase a number of acres just over the Woodstock line in the town of Hurley. There, White would begin to craft his own vision of a utopian art colony to be known as The Maverick. Ultimately, White's Maverick colony would lead to the Maverick Festivals, held each year between 1915 and 1931. Attracting, in its heyday, upward of five thousand people, Hervey White's festivals have been considered by many as an early precursor of the Woodstock Festival held in 1969.

While today's historians consider White's establishment of the Maverick colony as one of the more important chapters in Woodstock history, it is doubtful that few townspeople even took notice at the time. Instead, early in 1905, the town's attention was drawn to an unfolding scandal involving one of their own. For it was in February that the actions of Wittenberg's Frank Tone drew ample notice in the press and set the Woodstock gossip machine in motion. Tone, described by the *Kingston Daily Freeman* as a man of simple means, had found employment as a coachman in St. Remy for a wealthy

New Yorker. As Tone was soon to discover, much to his delight, his employer was the father of Mabel Hockridge. Despite their decidedly different stations in life, love would soon blossom between the coachman and the daughter as she became increasingly fond of carriage rides in the vicinity of her father's farm. Keeping their romance secret, Tone and Hockridge both managed a disappearing act on Friday, February 3. Traveling to either Kingston or Saugerties (the record is not clear), the two young lovers were married without the knowledge of either family. Upon learning of the elopement, a not-so-pleased Mr. Hockridge called on and dispatched detectives to find the young lovers. And while a visit by the detectives to Tone's relatives in Woodstock proved fruitless, the hard fact of the matter was that the deed was done, Miss Hockridge was now Mrs. Tone. On how the marriage would fare in the years ahead, little is known. However, based on the description of the affair in the *Kingston Daily Freeman*, one is left to wonder how happy the new bride might have been as Mrs. Frank Tone. As the *Freeman* offered, "Mrs. Tone is a pronounced brunette…strikingly beautiful. Tone is not considered by those who know him best to be a heavyweight, either intellectually, morally or physically."

With the type of scandal local gossip feeds on still fresh in their minds, Woodstockers would learn in March that their supervisor was about to embark on a journey that would fulfill his political dreams. Traveling to Kingston on March 2, Vactor Shultis joined his fellow Ulster County Republicans as they boarded a train to Washington, D.C. There, the local Republicans would join fellow party members from across the nation to celebrate Teddy Roosevelt's inauguration as president of the United States. Staying at the capital's Hotel Dumbarton, the delegation from Ulster County arrived in Washington ready to march in the inaugural parade carrying, according to the *Freeman*, a "big stick" crafted from canvas and wood in tribute to Roosevelt's "walk softly and carry a big stick" slogan employed during his presidential campaign.

As spring moved into summer, it was announced that the actor Dan Sully had purchased the Irvington Hotel from Dr. Jacob Wurts. Dominating the center of town at what is now the intersection of Mill Hill and Rock City Roads, the Irvington served as a primary destination for Woodstock visitors until fire destroyed the building in 1932. Meanwhile, one of the highlights of the summer occurred in August, as hundreds representing different congregations from the area gathered at Riseley's Grove in Woodstock for a picnic and a temperance lecture on the Anti-Saloon League delivered by Reverend Henry Smith of Saugerties.

For most of 1905, however, the pace of news from Woodstock returned to reports of families visiting families, school events, who was ill and who might have died. Less than a month before blaring headlines talking of murder would sit atop the columns of various newspapers, perhaps the biggest news in Woodstock was the fact that G.W. Elwyn had butchered a rather fat hog. The animal was estimated at about 600 pounds, and, according to a brief note in the *Kingston Daily Freeman*, Elwyn had skillfully extracted 150 pounds of lard during the process.

Like most of Woodstock, Zena, in 1905, also moved at its own pace, seemingly without much on the horizon that would bring major concern. As residents of the hamlet moved through the year, a number of them would continue to support the temperance movement through their attendance at temperance concerts and lectures, such as the one held at the Methodist Church in May. At about the same time, it was also announced that Abbie Short would resign her position as the teacher at Zena's one-room schoolhouse. Change would also come regarding mail delivery when it was further announced that mail for Zena would now be delivered from Woodstock and not West Hurley. Meanwhile, Charles Shufelt would purchase a horse from Silas Brewer.

Zena had been the last of the hamlets incorporated into the Town of Woodstock. In large part, how Zena became a part of Woodstock was the result of political infighting that occurred during the second half of the nineteenth century. That infighting centered on a desire by county Republicans to carve up the Town of Kingston—a town, according to historian Alf Evers, controlled by Democratic politicians of Dutch and Palatine descent who used their "Irish lieutenants to take care of the quarry workers in times of need and expected their support on election day." As a result, with little opposition, the town's "bosses" were, as Evers offers, "able to wring remarkable profits from the place through every device known to corrupt politicians of the time."

Their efforts were indeed brazen, with little pretense. On election days, for example, Evers relates how "gangs of Irishmen marched in and surrounded the polls and prevented the voters of the opposition political machine from voting. There was violence and bloodshed." At the time, however, Republicans held the strings of power countywide and were determined to break up the bastion of local Democratic power. At the instigation of Republican leadership, local Republicans undertook a petition "calling for the annexation of the Town of Kingston's School district Number One to Woodstock." Citing, in the petition, that they had been "robbed of their elective franchise by a lawless gang of perjurers, ballot-box stuffers, jawbreakers, thieves and able-bodied paupers," Republicans gathered the support of the county's board of supervisors along with support from the state legislature to begin dismantling the Town of Kingston. As a result, the town was severed into three parts, with the area we now call Zena added to Woodstock, another section added to the Town of Ulster and the remainder left to exist as the current Town of Kingston.

As fall approached in 1905, the local paper noted that William Reynolds, proprietor of the Reynolds' Boarding House on Mead's Mountain Road, visited, along with his wife, Elizabeth, the home of John Harrison in Zena. The visit by Mr. and Mrs. Reynolds was not the first time that year the name of John Harrison is to be found in the public record, however. A major story in September would come to dominate concerns not only for the hamlet but also for all Woodstock, as a powerful storm swept through the area. As rain and wind impacted the town during the course of two days, Supervisor Vactor Shultis, isolated in his Bearsville home, would declare the storm the worse he had ever seen. According to an account

Floodwaters cover Woodstock's main road. *Courtesy Historical Society of Woodstock Archives.*

offered by Shultis to the *Freeman*, "The Sawkill rose rapidly in the few hours the rain fell, at one point the water rising nine feet in a remarkably short time." As a result, a fourteen-foot bridge in Shady was washed away, as was part of Dan Sully's raceway in Lake Hill. A blacksmith shop in Bearsville, according to the paper, was torn from its foundation as a "torrent of water coming down the stream was strong enough to tear a mammoth tree loose from the banks and carry it against the shop." Elsewhere in Woodstock, the storm was having a similar impact as "rain fell in sheets as almost to block out the landscape that the darkness had not hidden…in the village of Woodstock itself the wind blew like a hurricane, uprooting trees, breaking off huge branches and limbs and in a few places unroofing small barns and out buildings."

Meanwhile, in Zena, where, at the time, its two reservoirs supplied the city of Kingston with its drinking water, John Harrison was having his own problems. As overseer of the reservoir's well houses, Harrison arrived to find the buildings almost "closed with debris and that the water was the highest ever known." Below the Kingston No. 1 reservoir sat a two-story stone building where the "water from both reservoirs is filtered before it's used by Kingstonians." The power of the storm and the rain it brought, however, forced the rising water and debris inside the building, creating a situation in which the filters had to be disconnected. Unable to travel to Kingston to inform officials there about the damage done, Harrison somehow found his way to Woodstock to telegraph the city that, as a result of the damage, the residents of the City of Kingston would be drinking unfiltered water until he and others from the city could make repairs.

One of two Zena reservoirs operated by the City of Kingston. *Courtesy Historical Society of Woodstock Archives.*

Working without rest during the days that followed, Harrison was eventually able to contain and repair the damage caused by the storm. Once again, Kingston's water supply was safe to drink, a fact noted by the local press with credit to Harrison given.

As a well-respected man in Woodstock, John Harrison, like his neighbors, preferred to live quietly. Having his name in the newspaper, as it was following the storm, was not something he would have sought. Little did he realize that, before the year was out, the Harrison name would find itself inked in headlines in ways he could not imagine.

3
DECEMBER 5 AND 6, 1905

Tuesday morning, December 5, arrived with signs that a change of season was not far off. The temperature had dipped to 18 degrees during the early morning hours and it was doubtful the day would see the thermometer rise above freezing. And, though warmer temperatures were predicted in the coming days, winter was beginning to settle in the Woodstock valley.

As Charles Wolven, yet another employee of the City of Kingston reservoir system in Zena, was beginning to ready himself for the day ahead, there was a sudden pounding on his door. Opening it, Wolven found Cornell Van Gaasbeek on the other side. Wolven was confused at first by Van Gaasbeek's excited state, but the reason for his visitor's agitation soon became clear. Van Gaasbeek was asking that Wolven call John Harrison and tell him his son was dead. "He poisoned himself," Van Gaasbeek told Wolven. "And he lays in my house dead. He's all swelled up so you wouldn't know him."

As suddenly as Van Gaasbeek had arrived, he departed, leaving Wolven confused and not sure what to do. Possessing one of the early telephones in Woodstock, Wolven eventually placed a call to Harrison and attempted to explain to the father the encounter he just had with Van Gaasbeek. Harrison, living farther away from the scene than Wolven, asked if he would go to Van Gaasbeek's house and see what was going on. Wolven, still unsure what he should really do, appears to have hesitated and delayed in following Harrison's request. As a result, Van Gaasbeek returned and again asked Wolven that Harrison be called to come immediately. Wolven, who would later describe Van Gaasbeek as "perspiring freely, seemed badly frightened and greatly excited," assured Van Gaasbeek that the elder Harrison was on his way. With that, Van Gaasbeek again left in haste. It would be the last anyone would see him for two days.

By sheer coincidence, as Wolven continued to debate what to do, Dr. Mortimer Downer of Woodstock arrived at the Wolven home. On Wolven's relating the strange arrival of Van Gaasbeek to the doctor, Downer urged that both he and Wolven go to the Van Gaasbeek house at once. What they discovered on their arrival was reported later that day in the *Kingston Daily Freeman*:

> *Pushing in the front door, he* [Downer] *found that while it was not locked there was something against it. The obstacle was the body of young Harrison who lay stretched out on his back, his head against the door, his right hand above the head as though to fend off a blow and his left arm bent at the elbow so that the hand was at about his hip. His face was covered with blood and there were marks showing where several blows had been struck on his head. On the end of the sofa at his side lay an old battered hammer with hair adhering to it.*

Looking around a room that was approximately ten feet square and included a stove, a table and a few chairs, the pair noticed dirty dishes left on the table as if someone had departed quickly. A corncob pipe "lay on the floor with some of the ashes spilled out," while a turned-up carpet seemed to indicate a struggle had taken place.

The dead man lying on Van Gaasbeek's floor was twenty-year-old Oscar Harrison. The younger Harrison had only recently returned to Woodstock eleven days before, having, earlier in the year, left town after taking up with a traveling show titled *Silver's Peck's Bad Boy*, based on the popular series written by George Wilber Peck from the late 1800s through the early 1900s. The theme that ran through Peck's stories focused on a young boy, Hennery, who executed pranks on adults, including his father. In its depiction of these various pranks—some even sadistic by today's standards—*Peck's Bad Boy* came to symbolize growing societal fears at the time over the rise of juvenile delinquency. Such fears in the general dialogue may have accounted for an unfavorable description of the younger Harrison that appeared in the local press. During its first report on the murder, the *Kingston Daily Freeman* concluded in its last paragraph that "Harrison was a wild young man and had been in the habit of staying away from home at times."

On his return home, Harrison had renewed a previous association with Van Gaasbeek and his nephews. There was some speculation at the time that the reason he did so was to help prove that Van Gaasbeek and the Conines were responsible for the recent theft of chickens in town. Unfortunately, for Harrison, as a result of his past association with Van Gaasbeek and the Conines, he, too, was viewed with some suspicion by a number of local residents. On the Saturday prior to his son's death, the senior Harrison, according to the *Freeman*, spoke to his son about the need to discontinue his association with Van Gaasbeek and the Conines and that, "if he could furnish any evidence of their guilt, lay it before the proper authorities." While it is not known if the advice of his father had any impact on the younger Harrison, it is known that, following dinner with his family, Oscar Harrison left his father's house. It would be the last time his family would see him alive.

AFTER VIEWING THE SCENE inside Van Gaasbeek's home, Downer returned with Wolven to his home. At approximately nine o'clock that morning, the Woodstock doctor placed a call to the coroner in Kingston informing him of what he had witnessed. As noted, murders simply didn't happen in Woodstock. Nor did they happen in Ulster County all that often. As a result, expectations about what, officially, would take place next were unclear. The coroner arrived in Woodstock around noon, Woodstock's Justice Elwyn issued a warrant for the arrest of Van Gaasbeek, and Woodstock's constable made a cursory attempt to locate the subject. Meanwhile, county officials—the district attorney and the sheriff—did not receive word of the murder until two o'clock that afternoon. That notification, however, did not arrive by means of official communication. Rather, it wasn't until a reporter from the *Kingston Daily Freeman* made an inquiry to their offices that they became aware of what had taken place in Woodstock and a response was mounted. As the *Freeman* noted, "The law does not seem to, in so many words, make it the specific duty of any of these officials promptly to notify the county officials, and probably 'what is everybody's business is nobody's business' explains the delay."

Assistant District Attorney Frederick Traver would, ultimately, arrive at the scene by four o'clock that afternoon. His first order of business was to prepare a list of possible witnesses. Unable to locate the Conines, who were assumed to have some knowledge of the events involving Van Gaasbeek and Harrison, Traver arranged warrants for their apprehension with Justice Elwyn. In addition, Traver went about securing the murder scene and ensuring that Harrison's body was properly cared for in advance of an autopsy that would be performed the following day.

Also arriving that afternoon was Under Sheriff Grove Webster Jr. Appointed by his father, Sheriff Grove Webster, in 1903, the junior Webster undertook arranging with constables from Woodstock and Saugerties a search for both Van Gaasbeek and the missing Conine family.

Later that evening, sometime after nine o'clock, the Conines were found to have returned home. Again, confusion appears to have reigned between the different authorities involved in the investigation. While it had been originally intended that the Conines were to be arrested and brought to Kingston for questioning, communication between the district attorney's office and the sheriff seems have been at cross purposes. As a result, questioning of the Conines took place at their house in Zena.

The story they told would serve to confirm what investigators were already assuming. It was Cornell Van Gaasbeek they really needed to find. According to the Conines, Van Gaasbeek had come to their home around ten o'clock the night before. Though Van Gaasbeek was related to the family—the Conine children were sons of Van Gaasbeek's sister—he had not been, they told investigators, in their home for some time. Entering their house that night, Van Gaasbeek, according to the Conines, stated that "he was afraid to go to his own home and went to sleep in a chair beside the stove." Early the next morning, while Arthur Conine was outside chopping wood, his brother George joined him. Though he would later offer a slightly different story, George told his brother, "I heard hard breathing in Cornie's house last night. Wonder what's the matter?"

A short time later, Van Gaasbeek emerged from the Conine house and, according to initial testimony, seemed nervous about returning to his home. It was also noted, presumably by Arthur, that George was acting strangely as well, "as if he knew more than he wanted to tell." At that point, George accompanied Van Gaasbeek next door to his own home, where they found the body of young Harrison.

Reformed Church in Woodstock, where the autopsy for Oscar Harrison was performed. *Courtesy Historical Society of Woodstock Archives.*

The following day, Wednesday, December 6, Coroner Cook conducted an inquest in Woodstock. As an essential element of the inquest, Dr. Henry Van Hoevenberg from Kingston, assisted by Dr. Downer, presented the results of the autopsy that had been performed on Harrison. In an odd twist to where the autopsy was performed, local undertaker Ira Bovee, believing his funeral parlor was too small, arranged for the autopsy to be conducted in the basement of the Reformed Church on Woodstock's Village Green.

As he testified, Van Hoevenberg spared no detail, offering, as reported in the *Kingston Daily Freeman*, that his examination of the victim's skull showed "several external contused wounds and three fractures of the skull, one on the right side right side above the right ear, one above the left ear and one on the forehead." Continuing, the doctor testified that he also "found under the fractures on the sides of the head over the ears extravasated blood and laceration of the brain substance. There were several contused wounds on the face, one on the hand and one on the back of the neck. The wounds on the head were made by some blunt instrument in my judgment," and, "up to this time the man had been dead forty hours." Van Hoevenberg would go on to offer that "Harrison had probably lived several hours after the injuries were inflicted." When asked for his conclusions, Van Hoevenberg stated, "the cause of death was laceration of the brain with extravasation of blood" and, "the wounds on the body could have been indicted with a hammer."

In addition to the autopsy report, further details were added to the record regarding what may have taken place outside the Conine home on the morning Harrison's body was discovered, primarily through the testimony of George Conine. Addressing the inquest, Conine stated that Cornell Van Gaasbeek was drunk when he came to their home on Monday evening. In addition, Conine offered a different story relating to what he had heard on the night in question. Rather than stating that he heard "hard breathing" coming from his uncle's house, Conine said that he heard a "funny noise" and thought it sounded like "stamping and kicking on the floor and groaning." When he asked Van Gaasbeek the next morning about the noise and suggested that he should go over to his house and see what was going on, Conine stated that Van Gaasbeek told him he was "afraid."

Quoting Conine directly, the *Freeman* printed the following testimony: "I said: 'I wouldn't be afraid to go to my own house.' He stood there for a minute and then looked excited, nervous and scared. After a little while he says 'maybe you better go along with me.' I stood a minute and then said: 'I'm not afraid to go along with you.' Then he started and I followed. He went to the front door of his house and I was behind. He pushed the door open about 18 inches and then stepped in sideways. I stuck my head in the door."

Conine continued, "Before I looked in the door he said: 'Look here, I guess he's dead.' Then he commenced to cry and said, 'What shall I do?' When I looked in I saw a body lying on the floor with his head towards the door. Did not look at his face. I turned as quickly as I could. When about half way to my house Van Gaasbeek yelled to me to hold on and said, 'George, what shall I do?' I told him, 'I don't know what you can do more than to go up to Mr. Wolven's and telephone his father.' He says, 'that's what I suppose I better do.'" Conine then concluded, "I saw him going up the road towards Wolven's before I went into the house."

Returning to his own house, George Conine was in the process of telling Emma Smith what had happened when Van Gaasbeek entered. According to Conine, Van Gaasbeek, as if speaking to no one, said, "Oh dear, I don't know what to do." At that point, Conine told Van Gaasbeek he had to leave and get to Woodstock. After going to his cellar to store some groceries, he met Van Gaasbeek outside. "I'm going away," Van Gaasbeek told him. "No use of me to stay here. I don't think I can do any good." With that, the two separated and went their different ways. Conine, too, had not seen his uncle since.

Finally, Conine offered additional information before the inquest that had not been previously reported. After he had left his uncle following the discovery of Harrison's body, Conine, on his way to Woodstock, stopped by Charlie Wolven's house to tell him of an interaction he had witnessed between Harrison and Van Gaasbeek the day before.

Wolven, who had been brought into the story through no desire of his own, listened as George Conine told him, "Monday about dinner time I went to the well for a pail of water and heard some angry words between Van Gaasbeek and Harrison," Conine continued: "I saw them in front of their house. 'Corny' was shaking some carpet. They were quarrelling when I went into the house."

Other witnesses were also called before the inquest. Hiram Conine offered that Van Gaasbeek not only seemed "worried and uneasy" but also "went out several times" on Monday night.

Ida Van Etten, owner of a local establishment known as the Klondyke, testified that Van Gaasbeek had come to her home on Monday evening. She

Zena Cemetery, where Oscar Harrison was laid to rest. *Author's collection.*

stated that "he was badly intoxicated," seemed "uneasy" and kept repeating, "I suppose that I'll have to go, but I dread it." Van Gaasbeek left her house at "about 8:30," she told the inquest.

At the conclusion of the day's testimony, Coroner Cook issued a burial permit. With the body released, the Harrisons began planning a funeral for their son. His final resting place would be in the Zena Cemetery, a short distance from the family home.

4
THE CHASE

Cornell Van Gaasbeek was not an educated man, but fifty-five years of living in a white man's world instinctively told him that when a young white man, the son of a well-respected member of the community, is found dead in the home of an unemployed black man suspected of theft, authorities would arrive at only one conclusion. Understanding what that conclusion would be led Van Gaasbeek to consider the only course of action open to him—get out of town.

Somewhere along the line, as witness lists and subpoenas were being prepared, as an autopsy was performed and an inquest held, attention finally turned to the whereabouts of Van Gaasbeek. Though the early delay in the arrival of authorities would, seemingly, have given Van Gaasbeek an ample head start, the color of his skin in a predominantly white Woodstock would, eventually, prove problematic. That said, even though he was seen in Woodstock shortly after the body of Oscar Harrison was first discovered, where he was almost twenty-four hours later was anyone's guess.

So it was that Woodstockers entered an uncomfortable period of time, facing the possibility that a murderer was somewhere among them.

Enter a man by the name of Everett Roosa.

Roosa (early print accounts presented his last name as Rose) was a mechanic and "engineer" by trade. He was also a self-proclaimed detective/investigator with no real professional connection to local law enforcement. Instead, it seems that Roosa's "expertise" came, primarily, from being an avid reader of Sherlock Holmes mysteries. In fact, he would readily boast that he had read everything Conan Doyle had ever written.

While Roosa was unaffiliated with the legal system, he obviously had connections with members of the county's sheriff's department. And, with the limited resources available to them, authorities encouraged Roosa to provide what assistance he could in locating Van Gaasbeek.

And so his quest began. On the very night the body of Harrison was found, Roosa had begun his search by staking out the none-too-savory Woodstock establishment owned by Peter and Ida Van Etten known as the Klondyke, a place Van Gaasbeek was known to have visited frequently. A long, cold night of waiting and watching proved fruitless, however, and Wednesday morning found Roosa visiting Van Gaasbeek's home in Zena to conduct his own search. While there, and permitted by authorities to ramble through Van Gaasbeek's house at will, Roosa came across a letter from another of Van Gaasbeek's sisters who lived in Saugerties. With thoughts that the suspect might have gone there to seek shelter and money, the would-be detective, in the company of Constable Ricks of Woodstock, began the trek to Saugerties on foot.

While an old letter wasn't much to go by, it was all Roosa had at the moment, and, if nothing else, Roosa was resolute when it came to following what clues he had. Walking with Ricks, the two followed the Glasco Turnpike, so named as the route once taken when the old glass factory in Shady would ship products to the Hudson River port in Saugerties. The road would later be used by bluestone companies working along the base of Overlook Mountain to transfer bluestone slabs to the neighboring town for shipment south to New York City.

As the two traveled and neared one of Woodstock's one-room schoolhouses, the Daisy School, Roosa had a thought. In what would later be described by the *Freeman* as his "Sherlock Holmes moment," Roosa wondered if one of the children might have seen Van Gaasbeek in the area or, at least, know something of him.

When both Roosa and Ricks entered the schoolhouse, no doubt Miss Darbee, who had been hired to teach at the Daisy School only in August of that year, was surprised by their presence. Nevertheless, intent on his mission, Roosa, as reported by the *Kingston Daily Freeman*, politely requested "of the pretty school madam that he be permitted to ask a question of the pupils and permission being granted, Roosa gave a description of Van Gaasbeek and asked if any of the children had seen him lately. One little girl raised her hand and timidly stated that her father had seen the Negro on Tuesday about 11 o'clock going up the slope of the Overlook, heading to Will Ploss's house."

Early dirt road leading up Overlook Mountain. *Courtesy of Historical Society of Woodstock Archives.*

With the new information in hand, the two-man search party switched direction and pressed up Overlook Mountain. Attempting to make sense of the multiple combinations of "wood roads and quarry roads," however, the two began to lose their way. Frustrated, Ricks and Roosa separated, and Roosa forged on alone, eventually finding his way to the Ploss home. Learning that Van Gaasbeek had indeed been there but had moved on, Roosa, zigzagging across the mountain's steep slope, began seeking out others who lived nearby. At Luther Cashdollar's, there had been no sighting. Tracing his route back, Roosa encountered a "German woman" who told him a "Negro had been at the house at 5:00 Tuesday evening and asked for something to eat." Being refused, he had gone on his way. At a home tucked back off the path he traveled, Roosa learned that "the Negro had spent Tuesday night and said he was going to Tannersville."

Passing through West Saugerties and continuing his Holmesian technique of interviewing children as he went, Roosa came to understand that his suspect had headed in the direction of Palenville in Greene County. By this point, having not slept all night and with some twenty miles of walking behind him, our Sherlock wannabe hired a horse and

Early street scene in Purling, New York. *Author's collection.*

driver to take him to Palenville. Once there, Roosa learned that his quarry still remained ahead of him, having moved on to Kiskatom, in the town of Catskill. As Roosa traveled on, he passed through the town of Purling, leaving strict instructions at the local post office that should Van Gaasbeek be seen to notify him immediately at his next stop in Cairo. It proved to be an important request, for no sooner had he arrived in Cairo than he was informed, as he entered the Cairo Hotel, "your man is in the Purling Post Office. They just telephoned."

Having worn out the horse he had hired earlier, Roosa commandeered another, and, "whirling the rig around, he drove as fast as possible to Purling," where, sitting in the post office, he found his Moriarty.

> Roosa: *"Hello Corn."*
> Van Gaasbeek: *"Hello."*
> Roosa: *"Corn, I want you."*
> Van Gaasbeek: *"What for?"*
> Roosa: *"You know."*
> Van Gaasbeek: *"What does this mean?"*
> Roosa: *"You know. I want you to go back and explain how Oscar Harrison got killed."*

After Roosa conducted a brief search of his suspect, finding only an old jackknife and noticing no bloodstains or marks on Van Gaasbeek, the two began the return journey to Ulster County. By the next morning, Cornell Van Gaasbeek was in a jail cell adjacent to the Ulster County Courthouse in Kingston. Continuing to maintain his silence, Van Gaasbeek's only request was to ask for the only lawyer he knew, a childhood acquaintance named Augustus H. Van Buren.

5
AUGUSTUS H. VAN BUREN

Enter Augustus H. Van Buren.

In Harper Lee's *To Kill a Mockingbird*, Atticus Finch is questioned by his daughter, Scout, wondering why her father has taken on the difficult challenge of defending Tom, a black man, against the word of a white woman.

Scout asks,

> *"If you shouldn't be defendin' him, then why are you doin' it?"*
> *"For a number of reasons,"* said Atticus. *"The main one is, if I didn't I couldn't hold up my head in town, I couldn't represent this county in the legislature, I couldn't even tell you or Jem not to do something again."*
> *"Atticus, are we going to win it?"*
> *"No, honey."*
> *"Then why?"*
> *"Simply because we were licked a hundred years before we started is no reason for us not to try to win,"* Atticus said.

Fiction often introduces us to characters who rise to levels beyond what is attainable by mere mortals. Such well-known characters as Atticus Finch tend to represent the pinnacle when it comes to living a life guided by a true moral compass and, despite the naysayers, accomplishing the hard task of maintaining self-respect through consistent and honorable actions.

Without stating the obvious, real life isn't quite so easy. No person is without flaws. And yet, in 1905, about as good an example or embodiment of the principles espoused by Lee's Atticus Finch, Augustus H. Van Buren, walked back into the life of Cornell Van Gaasbeek. At the time, neither could have foreseen the long road they were about to travel together.

A descendent of Tobias and Helena Bogardus Van Buren, who first arrived in Kingston in 1720, Augustus Van Buren's lineage and résumé speaks to an accomplished and well-respected resident of the area. Born in 1856 and, following an early education in the Kingston schools of the day, Van Buren went on to read law in the Kingston law firm of Charles Fellows. He was admitted to the bar in 1877. Two years later, Van Buren married Catherine McKinstry. Four children would follow, one daughter and three sons. In 1889, he joined with former state senator John J. Linson in the practice of law in Kingston.

Augustus H. Van Buren. *Courtesy of the Ulster County Clerk's Office.*

More than just a lawyer, however, Van Buren was also a perennial and integral insider when it came to local government and politics. A lifelong Democrat in a Republican county, there was little chance, for example, that he would be joining Woodstock's Vactor Shultis in attending Teddy Roosevelt's inauguration. That said, Van Buren would serve two terms as an alderman in Kingston, acted as counsel for the Ulster County Board of Supervisors and, between 1902 and 1906, served as corporation counsel for the City of Kingston.

Despite his obvious connections to the close-knit world of local politics and power, Van Buren was not someone who simply went along just to get along. A man of principle in a world where not all actions met the highest of standards, Van Buren was often at odds with the very powers he worked with. Such was the case when the county's Democratic Party met for its annual county convention in October 1905.

On October 3 of that year, the headline in the *Kingston Daily Freeman* read, "Augustus Van Buren Succeeds Cloonan—Is the Chief High Priest of Reform in Ulster County." Continuing with a not-so-veiled shot at Van Buren, the story's first paragraph opens:

Ever since announcement was made that John F. Cloonan was to forsake this city, leaving the post of chief reformer vacant, speculation has been rife as to who would play Elisha to Mr. Cloonan's Elijah? The question was settled in the Democratic county convention today when it became apparent that not only has the mantle of Mr. Cloonan fallen upon Corporation Counsel A.H. Van Buren, but that the garment is a fit.

The "high priest of reform" title attributed to Van Buren came from his attempt at the convention to put forward a resolution calling for a committee that would, "without regard to politics, take such steps as such committee so appointed deems advisable, to the end that the legality and necessity of the amounts presented to the board of supervisors for audit be inquired into and the amount of taxes to be levied be reduced to the lowest limit." In short, something wasn't quite right with the numbers, so let's investigate the board of supervisors and lift some of the burden off the shoulders of the taxpayer. In support of his resolution, Van Buren rose and offered an emotional assessment on the "poverty stricken condition of the county" and the need to bring relief to the taxpayer through "retrenchment." Then, turning his attention to the politicians gathered that evening and to the candidates who had been nominated by the convention, he challenged those in attendance by calling for a confession, a confession that would admit "that the Democratic Party in this county is in a hopeless minority and that the ticket nominated tonight does not stand the ghost of a chance of election." Tensions rose in the room as Van Buren was met with shouts of "throw him out!" Ignoring the calls for his ouster, he continued, "If we were to swing back to the days when we won elections, something will have to be done. We cannot win unless we stand for something. This is true in the nation and the state, as well as the county."

As Van Buren took his seat, sarcastic opposition by those who felt they had been directly challenged by Van Buren's resolution became the order of the evening. Everett Fowler, offering the primary rebuttal to Van Buren's remarks, rose to declare:

We all know that of all the reformers this state or the United States ever produced, Augustus H. Van Buren is the greatest—when he didn't have a chance to get on the inside. I am in favor of the resolution, although it will have no more weight than the clouds passing through the sky that tomorrow will have disappeared. I am in favor of an investigation that will go back ten years—yes twenty years, and then we will know who the great

> *reformers are, and among them all we will find no greater reformer than Mr. Augustus H. Van Buren. I am in favor of the resolution, although I have never yet posed as a reformer. My experience with a reformer has been that whenever a reformer comes to me and talks reform I place both hands on my pocketbook in order to keep the few pennies I may have there safe."*

Van Buren would respond simply with the fact that he "did not charge Mr. Fowler or the Board of Supervisors with anything, but if Mr. Fowler saw fit to put that construction on it—he might."

Fowler would not be silenced. Concluding that the whole proceeding was mere "bluster and bluff and did not amount to anything," he went on to charge that the only reason the resolution was offered was "because it looked good and would make good reading in the *Freeman*. When the *Freeman* comes out tonight it will say: 'At last the Democratic party have posed as reformers and the chief reformer is Augustus H. Van Buren. Thank God, the country is saved.'" Fowler would conclude his attack by offering to serve as "the lowest corporal in Brigadier General Van Buren's ranks as he poses as the g-r-r-r-and reformer of Ulster county."

Van Buren's resolution passed. The reformer prevailed.

Coincidently, as can happen in small towns, Fowler and Van Buren would eventually join together as legal partners representing New York City in the purchase of lands related to the construction of the Ashokan Reservoir.

Van Buren, well grounded in his principled ways, was not one to gladly suffer those who, because of their own prominence and self-importance, attempted to manipulate the levers of power to gain advantage over others. While a strong believer in ensuring that the law was the rightful means in resolving conflict or disputes, he was an even stronger believer that the law should not be used to trample on those without privilege or lacking the resources to support their rightful

Everett Fowler. *Courtesy of the Ulster County Clerk's Office.*

claims. Such was the case when, as corporation counsel for the City of Kingston, he went against the efforts of his own employer to deny the rights of Woodstockers as Kingston began to secure control of Woodstock's Cooper Lake for its municipal water supply.

Following the creation of the Kingston Water Department in 1895, Kingston began to seek a backup system for its Zena-based water supply. (Yes, this was the same Zena system John Harrison worked for.) Eventually, the city settled on Cooper Lake along with tapping the Mink Hollow stream through a mile-long, twelve-inch pipe. As a result, to ensure protection of the system, the City of Kingston began to exert increasing, unilateral control over Woodstock's waterways—sometimes with the agreement of property owners, sometimes not. As Alf Evers described in his history of Woodstock, "There had been no public discussion or consultation with Woodstock people as a whole. That helped explain why a good many people resented the taking over of rights in their water by their bigger and stronger neighbor." Those concerns extended to property owners both upstream and downstream from the lake.

At the time Kingston began to exercise its control, Cooper Lake existed on a much smaller scale than we know today. Originally carved out through glacial activity, the lake was expanded by the City of Kingston over the years, and the height of the dam constructed to hold back its waters was increased. While the dam itself caused concerns for those Woodstockers whose homes sat perched below, the restricted flow of water into the Sawkill Creek, now controlled by the city, also proved to be a problem for working mills situated downstream from the lake's output.

As a result of the seeming lack of concern for those impacted by the city's actions, litigation was first initiated in 1901 against Kingston by Bearsville resident Elting Simpkins for "damages resulting from construction of the dam at the outlet of Cooper's Lake." Simpkins, who owned a sawmill along the Sawkill, claimed that, prior to work on the dam, water flow had been sufficient enough to permit his mill to operate. Following construction, however, as Simpkins offered in court, the flow of water was reduced enough to render his mill inoperable. Simpkins sued for $3,000. Despite a wait of four years—and legal opposition from Kingston—the court eventually sided in Simpkins's favor. According to a report in the *Kingston Daily Freeman* at the time, the judge held "that the storage of water in the manner in which the city stored it is unusual and irresponsible. The city undertook to impound the waters of Cooper Lake without first purchasing the rights of Mr. Simpkins or taking condemnation procedures to acquire his rights or to pay him damages."

Cooper Lake Dam. *Author's collection.*

Two years after Simpkins filed his lawsuit, neighbors along the Mink Hollow stream also found their way to the courthouse. There, legal representatives of property owners above the lake claimed that the tapping of Mink Hollow waters for diversion to Cooper Lake entitled them to damages because, during the summer months, "when they need water the most of all and the stream is at its lowest, the water is all taken away from them." Boardinghouses along the stream also got into the act, claiming that "the diversion of water has ruined trout fishing and therefore injured their businesses by making their houses less attractive to boarders."

Concern over such claims did not go unnoticed in the halls of official Kingston. Serving as corporation council in 1905—the same year he would take on Van Gaasbeek's defense—Augustus Van Buren offered in his year-end report to the city that seventeen actions had been brought against Kingston "to recover damages for the diversion of waters of the Sawkill Creek and the Mink Hollow stream." Noting that he had previously urged the city to utilize proper proceedings in such matters (as had the judge in the Simpkins case), Van Buren openly and directly warned the very government that employed him that "the parties who have brought these suits will, in my judgment, recover some damages."

Rather than listening to Van Buren's warnings and undertaking the corrective actions he recommended, some in the halls of power, according to Van Buren's own words, urged "that every such case be fought to the end no matter what merit it may have." Van Buren would not hear it. Rejecting the notion of bringing untoward pressure and financial hardship on those with legitimate claims, he responded officially, "Because the city can force a man who has not the money to fight a law suit to settle for less than is justly due him, is no reason why it should do so."

Ultimately, Van Buren was heard and the city, in the spring of 1906, appointed a committee to properly obtain additional rights around Cooper Lake and along the Sawkill.

While politics and the law were his primary vocations, Van Buren was also a man who pursued local history, social engagement and, perhaps his greatest love, life as a country farmer.

As a writer of history, Van Buren published *Ulster County under the Dominion of the Dutch* in 1923. Years later, another historian, Alf Evers, would offer praise for his effort, citing Van Buren's recognition of Native Americans as a people and a culture beyond the stereotypical images of savages that much of our earlier history presented. Writing in his own acclaimed history, *Woodstock—History of an American Town*, Evers observed, "It was not until 1923 when Kingston lawyer Augustus Van Buren in his *Ulster County Under the Dominion of the Dutch* could present the American Natives as other than cruel barbarians worthy of whatever barbarism was inflicted on them in return that at least there was recognition of how very barbaric the white Americans had been."

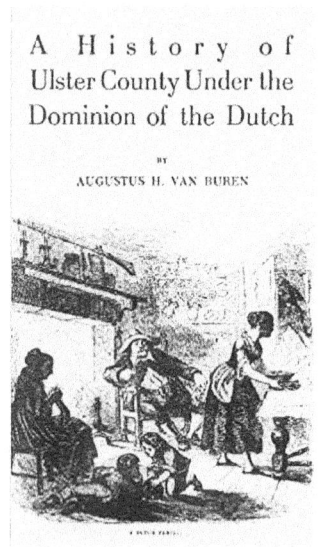

Book cover for Van Buren's history of the Dutch in Ulster County. *Author's collection.*

Though Van Buren conducted his legal and government business primarily in Kingston, he also owned a farm in the town of Gardiner, where he and his family would retreat as often as they could. There, in addition to his attempts to solve the mysteries of farming, he and Catherine would often entertain groups of visitors from Kingston. Van Buren's wife was active in a number of areas, including a variety of women's clubs that, in the late nineteenth and early twentieth centuries, saw rapid growth across America. Their purpose, in towns both large and small, varied from social, to literary, to political. Each club was as unique as the community in which it met, offering women the opportunity to voice opinions on the larger issues of the day. Topics often ranged from philosophy to history, from English poets to local charitable giving, from temperance to the right to vote for women. For women like Catherine Van Buren, such gatherings not only afforded solidarity but also offered the opportunity for women to expand their knowledge, to learn and give thought to issues and to otherwise broaden their awareness of the world despite limited educational opportunities and the inability to have their voices carry weight at the ballot box.

The Van Buren farm would, at times, serve as host to such groups. In fact, slightly more than two months before the murder of Oscar Harrison, the *Kingston Daily Freeman* printed this announcement:

> *The Lowell Club will hold its initiative meeting for the fall and winter of 1905–06 on Saturday of this week at Gardiner, the summer home of Mr. and Mrs. Augustus H. Van Buren. Each member of the club will have the privilege of inviting one guest. There will be reduced rates on the Wallkill Valley railroad for the club and its guests. The train leaves the West Shore station* [Kingston] *on Saturday at 8:55 a.m.*

Van Buren was proud of his farm. Able to employ workers to ensure its viability during his absence, the lawyer, politician and sometime historian attempted to seriously pursue his Shawangunk Hall Farm as a working concern. A 1911 advertisement for the M.B. Bookstaver Company in the *Kingston Daily Freeman* offers testament to the success of those pursuits.

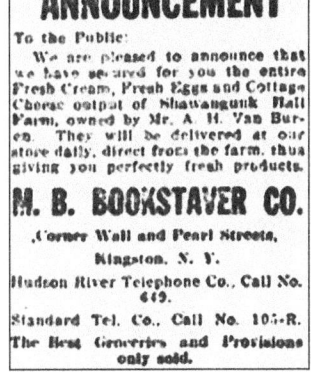

We are pleased to announce that we have secured for you the entire Fresh Cream, Fresh Eggs and Cottage Cheese output of Shawangunk Hall Farm owned by Mr. A. A. Van Buren. They will be delivered to our store daily, direct from the farm, thus giving you perfectly fresh products.

Advertisement in the *Kingston Daily Freeman* for products produced by Van Buren's farm. *Retrieved from digitized scan. HVRH website.*

With the seriousness of the farm's purpose noted, however, Van Buren was not above mocking his own skills as a farmer while, at the same time, giving credit to those he employed. During a presentation to the Rosendale Farmers Institute in 1908, Van Buren offered, as reported in the *Freeman*, his response to the question "Does Farming Pay?" The proprietor of Shawangunk Hall Farm began by stating emphatically, in response to the question, "No man in Ulster County is more competent than I am to express an opinion on the subject." Declaring that he would present examples of his "skills" as a farmer, Van Buren went on to regale the audience gathered by stating that he was a "scientific farmer" and would provide examples about his claimed expertise. "I started raising potatoes," he offered.

> *I planted whole potatoes, half potatoes, quarter potatoes and potatoes with one eye. My farmer John, placed sticks at the head of each row with the words "whole potato" or "half potato," or whatever the row contained on them. "Ah, John." I said, when he had finished, "that's fine. Now anyone can tell just what part of a potato is in each row." And then the sun shone and shone and shone. And then it rained, rained and rained for a thousand days, I think. And my clay soil got as hard as 40,000 blocks of granite. The sticks remained as monuments for the rows that were graves after all. From my half acre of potatoes, I got just two. They are in alcohol now.*

Wanting to share his experience with an early frost, Van Buren spoke of his fruit trees and his success until, "then came the frost." He continued:

> *One night in November, they held a convention in New Paltz. They're always holding conventions in New Paltz and no good ever comes of any of them. But one night, I remember it well, they held a convention in New Paltz, this is the absolute truth—all the jack rabbits on earth, they started for my farm. Hundreds of them, thousands of them, yes, I think there were a million of them. And the next morning out of my 250 fruit trees, hardly over 100 had any bark on them.*

Claiming that his dairy operation was what he knew most about, Van Buren also told the farmers gathered that night:

> *But if there is anything I'm strong on, its the dairy side of farming. Why my dear sirs, I know more about it than you would know if you lived to be 1,000 years. I know it all. And when my cows did not get along just right I*

said to farmer John: "John, did you ever-hear of 1-5-3 or something else?" "No, Boss, what's that?" asked John. "That's what those cows need John, is 1-5-3, and they're going to have it if it kills them and kills me. What these cows need is protein, that's it John. Those cows need protein." "Get some," I said. "We'll jam protein down one cow and carbohydrates down another, and we'll keep another on straight feed. We'll find out if these people know what they're talking about." So we tried it. After a while John came to me again and he said, "Boss, cow don't do well." "Give her more protein. John," I said, "that's what she wants, more protein." So John did the cow up in a ball and rammed more protein down her throat. The tears ran down the poor cow's face and finally she jerked loose, shot out of the door, jumped the Wallkill and went to New Paltz.

"Does it pay?" Van Buren asked the audience. And here he turned to the truths the land had long ago instilled in him and to the answer the question really posed for him.

When I take a train and come out to my farm I am in a different world. When I can feel the satisfaction of stamping my foot on the ground and saying this is mine, when I think that in that house my grandmother walked as a bride, that farm has been mine or my wife's family for 250 years, I am happier and all the money in the world cannot buy that recollection from me. I sit upon the porch and watch the sun go down. I am alone. And somehow I am purer and a better man. Does it pay?

As 1905 drew to a close and Van Buren began to prepare his defense of Van Gaasbeek, one last order of business required his attention. Having served as corporation counsel for the City of Kingston, his appointment was nearing an end. Due to exit the stage at the end of the year, he would not let the opportunity pass without some final words before the city's fathers.

On a Friday evening in December, Van Buren rose before Kingston's common council and both admonished and urged greater civic responsibility when it came to electing local officials. Speaking to the taxpayers of the city, he observed, according to the *Freeman*:

The fact is you get pretty nearly just the kind of government you deserve. In large measure, you are responsible for the very evil of which you complain. You grow red in the face over a political argument during a presidential canvas. You leave a comfortable home to go to a political meeting and yell like a lunatic in approval of the "hot air" of some "bellows" upon the platform. You tramp through the mud behind a brass band playing Tammany or the Roosevelt March. You do all these things during a presidential campaign, but when it comes to naming city officers, the management of city affairs, matters of more importance to you than forty presidential elections, a yoke of oxen can't get you to move. The expression, "He ain't fit to hold office," applied to city officials, is heard every day and has been heard ever since we have been a city. Well, you put him into office.

Augustus Van Buren was a successful and prosperous individual, born into a family that represented the history and heritage of the area. And it seems to have been that same history, a history he knew well, from which he drew the lessons he lived by: hard work, compassion for all, love of family, civic responsibility and the realization that victory can only come from a struggle hard fought.

So it was that, when Van Buren agreed to take up the defense of Cornell Van Gaasbeek, he understood the difficult path ahead. Not unlike Atticus Finch, Van Buren, too, would face the question why a man of his stature would take up the defense of a poor black man who was all but tried and convicted. In Van Buren's mind, the answer was fairly simple. The loss of self-respect that would come from abandoning all that he stood for and honored would not permit him to do otherwise. It wasn't so much that he sought praise from others; rather, he needed to be able to rise in the morning and look at himself in the mirror.

Van Buren also knew what Atticus Finch had known: the odds were already stacked against him. He understood that the long arm of America's original sin would eventually reach into the courtroom as he tried to defend a black man before an all-white jury. Still, as he sat on the porch of his farm watching the sun go down, he, too, may have assured himself, "Simply because we were licked a hundred years before we started is no reason for us not to try to win."

6
INTERLUDE

THE TRIAL APPROACHES

On Friday, December 8, Cornell Van Gaasbeek stood in a Kingston courtroom as an indictment against him for second-degree murder was read. According to the reporter's account in the *Freeman*, Van Gaasbeek never took his eyes off of District Attorney Frederick Stephan as the indictment was read. After reviewing the charges, Augustus Van Buren informed the court that the defendant would enter a plea of not guilty. With that, the brief arraignment was concluded and the case bound over to county court for trial.

By today's standards, the trial of Van Gaasbeek would move rather quickly following his arraignment. It would be little more than a month between the morning that Harrison's body was discovered and when jury selection began on January 9, 1906. With the holidays upon them, no doubt Augustus Van Buren and District Attorney Stephan felt the pressure of condensed time to prepare their respective cases. For Cornell Van Gaasbeek, however, held behind bars as Christmas and New Year's passed, each twenty-four hours that ticked by did so in slow motion.

In the interim, local racial tensions would flare and, as the result of an incident that unfolded only a short distance from where Van Gaasbeek sat in his cell, the spotlight on his case would only intensify.

Along Kingston's North Front Street, Markle's Saloon once operated. Noted for its frequent troubles, Markle's outdid even itself only a week following Van Gaasbeek's arraignment. As the headline in the *Kingston Daily Leader* blared on December 16, 1905:

> *A Desperate Fight*
> *Between Whites and Blacks at Markle's Saloon Saturday Night*

Claiming that the fight was the "worst fight ever seen on the thoroughfare," the report in the *Leader* pins its initial cause on a white man by the name of Vic Rogers. Upon entering Markle's, Rogers, noticing a group of black men also at the bar, is quoted as saying that it was "a——— (expletive deleted by newspaper) of a note for a white man to drink with a lot of damn Negroes." Noting that the black men already at the bar had a "grudge" against Rogers for "doing up Negroes" at another establishment earlier in the month, the newspaper account claims that the black men quickly "piled on" Rogers. As Rogers "went down and out," however, the report offers, "he put two of the Negroes out of his business."

From there, the fight moved outside and on to North Front Street. There, two other white men joined Rogers, and the two sides went at it "hammer and tongs." At one point, the black men managed to pull wooden slats from the stoop of the saloon and took to using them on Rogers and the others. The tide was turned, however, when the slats were taken from the black men and Rogers and his compatriots began to "beat them unmercifully."

Finally, local police arrived. They concentrated, as related by the *Leader*, on apprehending the black men first. "Tom Vandermark, colored, was arrested by Special Officer Cohen….Chief Hood and Policeman McIntyre went to the 'Hornet's Nest' in Higginsville* to arrest the other colored fellows." Eventually, Rogers would be arrested as well, but not without incident. As police were about to enter the courthouse with their prisoner

Higginsville street scene. *Author's collection.*

in tow, Rogers managed to break loose and flee. Finally recaptured by police—though "he fought desperately"—Rogers was returned to the courthouse, where a cell was waiting.

It was against such a backdrop—a backdrop that included a nation still well within the clutches of Jim Crow and where fifty-seven blacks had been lynched in the year that had just ended—that Augustus Van Buren prepared to defend his client. Van Buren hadn't gotten as far in life as he had, however, simply by expressing unbridled idealism. He was well aware that in the decade following *Plessy v. Ferguson* and its separate but equal doctrine, even in Upstate New York, whites held to certain beliefs and attitudes regarding the place a black man had in their community. Discrimination and white hierarchy were still the norm, not the exception. And although individuals such W.E.B. Du Bois and other black leaders were to found the Niagara Movement in 1905—which, four years later, would become the National Association for the Advancement of Colored People (NAACP)—Van Buren knew that the world he encountered every day would find it difficult to believe a black man's word when the death of a young white man was in question.

**Author's Note*: Higginsville was the name once given to what is now the Washington Avenue, Hurley Avenue area that leads out of Kingston toward the New York State Thruway. Some local residents may still recall it as the area that once included the viaduct over the Esopus Creek.

7
JURY SELECTION

Circumstantial evidence is a very tricky thing. It may seem to point very straight to one thing, but if you shift your point of view a little, you may find it pointing in an equally uncompromising manner to something entirely different.
—Sherlock Holmes in "The Boscombe Valley Mystery"

On Tuesday, January 9, Judge Charles Cantine called his courtroom to order. The trial of Cornell Van Gaasbeek was underway. Judge Cantine had been first elected to his position as county judge in 1904, following three terms as district attorney in Ulster County. A well-respected jurist, his family, not unlike Van Buren's, was well connected across the years. A descendent of Moses Cantine, a Huguenot leader from New Paltz, Judge Cantine graduated from Columbia Law School in 1882 and was admitted to the bar that same year. Cantine, again like Van Buren, was also a serious student of history and was known to offer numerous talks on a variety of historical topics. Noted for "a keen sense of justice," he was, as a jurist, also known for his ability to lose "sight of personalities in his search for the truth and the application of principle, both legal and moral."

At the table reserved for the prosecution sat District Attorney Frederick Stephan. No stranger to Van Buren, Stephan, similarly, was a well-respected attorney and politico in Ulster County. And, as the son of a former state legislator who, additionally, served as a trustee of the old Ulster Academy for eighteen years, the younger Stephan also maintained a strong family connection to the area. Born on May 29, 1859, Stephan graduated from

Left: Sketch of Judge Charles Cantine as it appeared in the *Kingston Daily Freeman* during the trial. *Retrieved from microfilm printout*. Kingston Library.

Right: District Attorney Frederick Stephan. *Courtesy of the Ulster County Clerk's Office*.

Union University at Albany Law School and was admitted to the bar in 1886. After building a successful law practice, he went on to serve as counsel for the Ulster County Board of Supervisors and, later, was elected to that same body, serving four years. Victorious in his campaign for district attorney in 1904, Stephan would serve at his post for the next three years before moving up to the bench himself as judge for Kingston's city court.

With quiet having descended over the courtroom, the potential jurors seated behind the defendant and the attorneys had to wonder what they were in for. For many, this would be their first experience with the criminal justice system, and more than likely, most hoped against hope that they wouldn't be selected. What was expected of them? What questions would they be asked? If they were selected, how long would the trial go on? And with court now in session, the gravity of what may be before them, no doubt, began to ebb its way into their thinking. This was a murder trial, and the defendant seated in front of them was accused of taking a human life.

As the lawyers began interviewing potential jurors, it became obvious that the matter of circumstantial evidence—and whether a juror could bring himself to convict on such evidence—would play an important role in the selection process. Without a witness who could directly testify to the fact that he or she saw Van Gaasbeek kill Harrison, could the prosecution string together a preponderance of indirect evidence that would lead a jury to conclude that Cornell Van Gaasbeek was guilty beyond a reasonable doubt? While an early juror was dismissed because he did not know what the term "circumstantial evidence" referred to, the prosecution also dismissed others when they firmly asserted that they could not convict on indirect evidence alone. James Ackerman, a farmer from Shawangunk, in response to a question from the district attorney about such evidence, stated, "Circumstances alter cases." And, no matter how strong that evidence might be, he did not think he could convict on that alone. Yet another prospective juror, David Stilwell from Lloyd, put it more bluntly: "A just verdict on circumstantial evidence would be not guilty."

Among the other jurors interviewed on that first day was former Woodstock supervisor Henry P. Van de Bogart. Van de Bogart would offer an interesting view when it came to the question of convicting—or not—on the basis of circumstantial evidence. In response to the question, the ex-supervisor stated that "he would have a prejudice against convicting a man of murder in the first degree on circumstantial evidence but would have no prejudice against circumstantial evidence in a case of murder in the second degree." Van de Bogart was ultimately dismissed because he lived "so near the scene of the alleged crime."

Since the jury that would be selected would consist of twelve white males, the question of racial prejudice also loomed large in the courtroom. For Van Buren, the problem of finding a white juror free of prejudice to judge the guilt or innocence of Van Gaasbeek was underscored during interviews with a number of potential jurors. When Paul Sheeley of the town of Denning was questioned, he stated that he was a man without prejudice. Questioned further on the matter of prejudice "against Negroes," Sheeley, described by the *Freeman* as "a farmer with profound pink and white whiskers such as seldom seen off the stage," stated that he had no problem passing "the time of day with one or to take a glass of beer with one just about as soon as with a white man." But, as the *Freeman* continued with his testimony, "he would not hire one as soon as a white man—not altogether because Negroes were not as good as workers as white men." Sheeley was dismissed.

Alfred Lyons from Rifton was presented with the same question concerning prejudice. Lyons, too, according to the *Freeman*, demurred in his initial answer, offering that the defendant's race would not influence him.

He subsequently added, however, that he "didn't think as much of a Negro as a white man." Whatever difference the lawyers saw between Sheeley and Lyons, however, is unclear, as Lyons was accepted as a juror.

By the time court recessed at noon that Tuesday, five jurors had been seated. They included, along with Lyons, Elvin Deyom, a druggist in Kingston with the nickname of "the Duke"; John Shiels of Warwarsing, a former policeman from New York who listed his occupation as farmer; Stephen Warren of Lake Katrine, listed as both a farm laborer and town clerk for the town of Ulster; and Levi Hasbrouck, a farmer also from Warwarsing.

Returning that Tuesday afternoon, Judge Cantine attempted to move both prosecutor and defense attorney toward completion of the twelve-man jury. David Freer, an Ellenville farmer, was selected as the sixth juror after Woodstocker Matthew Williams had been dismissed. The defense, possibly assuming too many connections with local law enforcement, peremptorily challenged former constable and former justice of the peace Ezra Sprague of Hardenburg. Similarly, District Attorney Stephan would challenge the next potential juror when the issue of circumstantial evidence once again became problematic. When asked about his feelings regarding such evidence by the prosecutor, James Ackerman from Shawangunk offered that he would have a problem finding the defendant guilty "no matter how strong" the circumstantial evidence might be. Similarly, Stephan would challenge two other potential jurors that afternoon, as they, too, found difficulty with the possibility of a conviction based on circumstantial evidence. As David Stillwell of Clintondale offered, in response to a question from Stephan, a true verdict in a case based on circumstantial evidence would be "not guilty." Similarly, David Sutton from the town of Lloyd told the court that he would not convict in a case based on circumstantial evidence.

As the afternoon wore on, the prosecution made most of the challenges that struck potential jurors. And, as more and more individuals were dismissed, the pool grew increasingly narrow. As it was, only five more jurors would be added at the end of a long day, one short of the twelve needed. Those additional jurors seated at session's end included Robert Fox of Shandaken; Erastus Rider from the town of Rochester; James Acker, a brickyard employee from East Kingston; Robert Sawyer from Warwarsing; and James Neise of Port Ewen. Jury selection for the day was ended when the prosecution dismissed the final available juror, Willis Scott Hayne Seager, a farmer from the town of Hardenbergh. His dismissal followed disclosure that he once served as a juror on a case of another black man, Elting Roe. As described by the *Freeman*, the Roe case was where "Mr. Van

Buren gained his place in the front rank of successful defenders of colored brethren in distress."

Unable to begin the trial of Van Gaasbeek that Tuesday, Judge Cantine, in an effort to complete the jury, ordered that twenty-four more jurors be called the next day.

When court was called into session on Wednesday, thirteen of the twenty-four jurors who had been called on short notice had found their way to the courthouse in uptown Kingston. While five were immediately excused for a variety of reasons, the second juror interviewed, Matthew Delanoy, was accepted. With Delanoy, a fisherman and keeper of fifty-five beehives, seated, Judge Cantine had his jury.

Thirty-four days after the body of Oscar Harrison had been found on the floor in Cornell Van Gaasbeek's house, the trial of the man accused of causing his death would now proceed.

8
TESTIMONY

The Ulster County Courthouse on Wall Street in Kingston speaks to the history of the area. It was, perhaps, a history that Augustus Van Buren knew better than most. As both a lawyer and a historian, Van Buren would have been well aware that it was on the very site the courthouse now occupied that the Constitutional Convention met in in 1777, creating New York State. Founded on a document written by John Jay, that same document would later serve as the foundation for the nation's own constitution. Nor could Van Buren have been unaware that a decade after the current courthouse was built in 1818, a former slave—who would eventually go by the name of Sojourner Truth—would become the first black woman to succeed in a legal case, a case that would see her son Peter freed following his illegal sale to an Alabama slave owner. The irony couldn't have escaped Van Buren. As he looked upon his own client, he had to wonder what fate would fall upon this black man.

At precisely 10:00 a.m. on that Wednesday, District Attorney Stephan stood before the jury and outlined the case he would bring against Van Gaasbeek. The defendant, he informed the twelve men before him, was charged with the murder of Oscar Harrison on December 5, 1905, without premeditation. As Stephan went on to describe the events leading up to the murder and the subsequent actions Van Gaasbeek took that day, the defendant, the lone black man in a sea of white principles, could only stare straight ahead as Stephan prepared to call his first witnesses.

Woodstock's Infamous Murder Trial

Ulster County Courthouse. *Courtesy Friends of Historic Kingston.*

Beginning with testimony from John Harrison, the deceased's father; Dr. Mortimer Downer, the Woodstock physician who was first on the scene; and Charles Wolven, the Kingston City Reservoir employee who was first confronted by Van Gaasbeek, the jury was treated to accounts describing the events on the morning Oscar Harrison's body was discovered. Harrison's father related to the jury how Oscar had left home on the Saturday evening before his death and had not returned. The next time he saw his son was when he was summoned to Van Gaasbeek's house, only to find Dr. Downer and Charles Wolven already there as his son lay dead on the floor. In offering his painful recollection of the scene he found, Harrison told how his son was lying on his back, "the right arm raised and the left arm by the side. There was blood coming from the nose and the mouth." In describing the interior of the house, Harrison noted, according to the *Freeman*, that "the room was in disorder. The carpet was disarranged. There was a table with some dirty dishes. A pipe with ashes lay on the floor." Concluding, Harrison also noted that he saw his son's coat hanging on the wall while, close to the body, "laid a hammer."

As he approached his examination of the witness, Van Buren seems to have been at cross-purposes. Certainly, he did not want to attack a man whose son, only a month before, had been brutally murdered. At the same time, it appears the defense was interested in establishing a picture for the jury that Oscar Harrison was no saint. Van Buren's initial questions elicited from the father a general description of his son: twenty years old; unmarried; five feet, eight or nine inches tall; and weighing about 140 pounds. On further questioning from Van Buren, according to the *Freeman*, Harrison told the jury that Oscar had left school when he was sixteen or seventeen years old and took up working for his uncles in Woodstock, though not continuously. At times, the father admitted, Oscar could also "be home doing nothing." Harrison also related how earlier in the year his son had taken up with the traveling show that had passed through Woodstock, returning three weeks later. After his return to Woodstock, Oscar, according to his father, would take "his meals occasionally but would be away during the day and sometimes nights." His father also told the jury that his son smoked and that he "never saw him drunk, but heard he drank." Finally, the elder Harrison offered that he had seen his son with the defendant at different times in Woodstock but had never witnessed him with any member of the Conine family.

Dr. Mortimer Downer was the next witness called to the stand by the prosecution. While Downer offered a description of the scene in Van Gaasbeek's house similar to that given by John Harrison, he added a few details not previously disclosed. Downer noted that there was "one spot of blood on the floor and three spots on the stairway, on the third or fourth step." He also explained that, in addition to several wounds on the face and head of Harrison, there were three wounds on his hands, "as though made by blows." In addition, while identifying the hammer found at the scene, Downer recalled that he, too, noticed a corncob pipe lying near the victim.

On cross-examination, the Woodstock doctor further testified that it was his opinion that Harrison had been struck on the head and "probably fell where he was found." Believing that Harrison had "possibly lay unconscious for three hours after being struck and before death," Downer estimated that the victim had been dead some "12 to 16 hours when found." Under additional questioning by Van Buren, Downer told the court that he had known Van Gaasbeek several years and had never known him to be a problem in the community and that he "always found him gentlemanly and nice acting." The witness further related that while he had known Oscar Harrison for about five years, he had never seen both Van Gaasbeek and Harrison together. And, while he had also known members of the Conine family for a number of years, he had never seen Harrison at their home.

Following Dr. Downer, Dr. Henry Van Hoevenberg took the stand to review and affirm the findings of the autopsy he had performed on Harrison's body in the basement of the Reformed Church. Declaring that death had occurred due to a fractured skull, Van Hoevenberg described four contused wounds on the head and one he found on the back of Harrison's neck. In a bizarre bit of courtroom drama, the skull of the victim was produced and the injuries shown to the jury. As Van Hoevenberg explained the wounds, according to a description provided in the *Kingston Daily Freeman*, "morbid curiosity seekers who crowded the courtroom stretched their neck and trod on one another's toes to get a view of the gruesome exhibit."

During cross-examination, Van Hoevenberg also expanded on the previous estimate given by Dr. Downer, explaining that Harrison "had lived some time after receiving the blow to the head and one which had been found on the back of Harrison's neck—probably five or six hours longer."

As Stephan concluded his questioning of the witness, Van Buren rose to ask Van Hoevenberg why there was no evidence of a skull fracture externally on the left side of the head, though a fracture was evident once the scalp was removed. Here, both Van Hoevenberg and Dr. Downer, who was later recalled, seemed uncertain. Van Hoevenberg attributed it to the possibility that Harrison had fallen and that the fracture occurred when his head hit the floor. Downer suggested the idea that the reason the blow on the left side of the head failed to show was due to the fact that Harrison had been wearing a hat when the blow was struck. With that answer, Van Buren decided to take the gloves off when it came to the good doctor from Woodstock. Following a statement by Downer that he had, in his practice, encountered five cases involving a fractured skull, Van Buren asked him to discuss each case. When Downer replied that four of the five cases had been in Woodstock proper, Van Buren sarcastically offered as an aside, "Woodstock must be a great place for broken skulls."

Van Buren's remark would be about as far as he would go during the course of the trial when expressing frustration or skepticism. Nor would he attempt to unnecessarily embarrass a witness before the jury despite his feelings about the veracity of their testimony. No doubt, too, in the case of Dr. Downer, Van Buren was well aware of the physician's reputation in the community. To push the witness beyond the facts he had to offer through further derision might not have gone well with the assembled jurors. Downer, having arrived in Woodstock in 1898, would go on to faithfully serve the area for the next twenty years. It is even quite possible that, as a member of the staff at Kingston's Benedictine Hospital, the paths of

Downer and some members of the jury might have crossed during his service there. A graduate of Columbia University's College of Physicians and Surgeons in 1896, Downer would be described in the *Freeman* as "one of the best known physicians in Ulster County," and that "he was always vitally interested in the welfare of Woodstock and always active in working for the best interests of the village."

As the morning session moved into the afternoon, District Attorney Stephan brought forth one of his prime witnesses, Van Gaasbeek's own nephew, George Conine, who, as he explained to the jury, lived with his father; two brothers, Albert and Arthur; and Emma Smith. As reported in the *Freeman*, "George Conine, Negro, testified that he lived in the house near Van Gaasbeek's house" and went on to establish the presence of Harrison at Van Gaasbeek's home on the day of the murder. "I saw Oscar Harrison at Cornell Van Gaasbeek's house about dinner time. He stood by the door," Conine testified. He further told the jury, "I saw Harrison again about 3 o'clock that afternoon. I was in the yard near the corner of the house and he stood about 100 feet from Van Gaasbeek's house. He was not walking around but standing still. No one was near. He was alone. I did not see Oscar alive after that."

On further questioning from the district attorney, Conine delivered an even more dramatic element to the case against Van Gaasbeek. Noting that it was a cold night when he [Conine] finally returned home, the witness told the jury that he had gone outside to retrieve some dry wood for the fire. Explaining that he walked halfway between the two houses where there was some "hickory brush," Conine recalled: "As I was breaking it up I heard a groaning noise and like somebody stomping around the floor. I listened for a minute and went into [my] house."

After tending to the fire and eating his dinner, Conine related that "between 10 and 11 o'clock Cornell Van Gaasbeek came in, stood by the stove warming himself, got a chair, sat down and went to sleep." The following morning, Conine offered, though he wanted to get ready for work, Van Gaasbeek was still at his house. Continuing his testimony as reported by the *Freeman*, Conine then related a conversation he claimed to have had with the defendant that morning:

> Conine: "Uncle Corny, if I was you I'd go over home and see what went on at your house last night. I heard very strange noises there."
> Van Gaasbeek: "I'm kinder afraid to go up there after what you say."
> Conine: "That's strange. Afraid to go to your own house? I'll go with you."

Approaching the house, according to Conine's testimony, Van Gaasbeek found the door would not open all the way. Squeezing through what opening there was, Conine testified that his uncle, once inside, shouted, "He's dead. Look here, he's dead."

Looking in, Conine explained, he could see only a leg and a foot. Feeling there was nothing else he could do, he returned to his house, only to be followed by his uncle calling after him. "George, what shall I do? What shall I do?"

"I don't know," Conine responded, "unless you telephone to his father." With that, Conine returned to his house and prepared to head to work. Before he left, however, he told the jury that Van Gaasbeek commented to him, "It was a strange thing for that boy to poison himself in his own house." Apparently, that would be the last conversation Conine would have with his uncle; he concluded, in response to Stephan, that that would be the last he saw of his uncle the rest of the day.

With Conine's testimony fresh in their memories, Judge Cantine brought the day's proceedings to an end and dismissed the jurors for the evening.

The next morning, George Conine returned to the stand. Taking a different line of questioning, District Attorney Stephan began to explore Van Gaasbeek's physical and emotional state on the day of the murder. Conine's testimony, along with that of others who would follow him to the stand that morning, would drive an additional nail into the defendant's legal coffin. Leading with the headline "Three Stages of Inebriety," the *Freeman* reported that Conine described to the jury that, over the course of the day prior to discovering Harrison's body, his observations of his uncle were that "He was intoxicated"; "He was drunk"; "He was drunker yet."

First to offer corroboration of Conine's assessment of the defendant's sobriety that day was thirteen-year-old Sarah Wolven, daughter of the same Charles Wolven on whose door Van Gaasbeek first knocked on the morning young Harrison was found dead. The younger Wolven testified that on the day the death was discovered, she encountered the defendant as she was returning home from school. Stating that Van Gaasbeek was heading in the direction of Woodstock, Wolven observed, as their paths crossed, that Van Gaasbeek was "intoxicated" and that he "staggered."

Apparently, according to further testimony, Van Gaasbeek—whatever his condition might have been—made his way to the village of Woodstock that afternoon. Nicholas Dibble, who operated the Disch Mill (located where the Woodstock Golf Club is today), testified that he had seen Van Gaasbeek at the mill on the afternoon in question and that "he staggered." Henry Longendyke, also at the mill that day, corroborated Dibble's testimony.

Former site of Disch's Mill, now the Woodstock Golf Club. *Courtesy of Historical Society of Woodstock Archives.*

To follow along the same line of questioning, the prosecution also called both Peter and Ida Van Etten to the stand. Testifying that Van Gaasbeek arrived at his home around 6:30 on Monday evening, Peter Van Etten told the court that the defendant "staggered" as he took a chair. Van Etten went on to describe the conversation that followed. Claiming that Van Gaasbeek asked him to come and cut some stone for him, Van Etten, instead, observed, "You're quite drunk." Van Gaasbeek replied, "Do you think so?"

At this point in the *Freeman*'s account of Van Etten's testimony, the reporter speculates that, perhaps, the prosecutor wanted more from the witness than he had yet given. "The District Attorney," offered the *Freeman* reporter, "seemed to expect testimony of a more important conversation from this witness, but did not get it, although he asked repeatedly." Finally, according to the paper's account, Stephan "asked point blank about what was said as Van Gaasbeek was leaving?" Van Etten replied that the defendant said, "There's no use to dread it, I might as well go on."

What might Van Gaasbeek be dreading? That was the question the prosecution left in the minds of the jurors as Peter Van Etten concluded his testimony. Was he dreading going home knowing full well that the badly beaten body of Oscar Harrison lay on the floor of his cabin? Or, was he referring to something else?

Recognizing the implication such testimony might have on the jury, Van Buren rose to cross-examine and to counter the impression left by Van Etten's testimony. After establishing that it was not unusual for Van Gaasbeek to visit the Van Etten home, Van Buren also had the witness note that Van Gaasbeek, upon arriving, had spoken of how cold it was that night. In response to a question from Van Buren, Van Etten conceded that he "supposed he [Van Gaasbeek] referred to dreading the cold" and going out in it.

To further establish Van Gaasbeek's lack of sobriety that day, the prosecution also brought Peter Van Etten's wife, Ida, to the stand. Here, for a brief bit, the *Freeman*'s trial reporter transitions into the paper's fashion reporter. Describing Ida Van Etten as she took the stand, the reporter offered that she "wore gold rimmed spectacles and a large black picture hat trimmed with white ribbon." Corroborating her husband's testimony, Ida Van Etten testified that Van Gaasbeek was at their home when she returned on the evening in question. In response to questions from Stephan, though she couldn't quite remember all that she talked to Van Gaasbeek about, she noted that the defendant was indeed intoxicated. She further offered that he "walked back and forth and seemed uneasy." Describing how he went to their window a couple of times, the witness also confirmed that Van Gaasbeek was reluctant to leave. Using the same words as her husband, she testified that Van Gaasbeek said more than once that he "dreaded it."

Countering once again, Van Buren questioned Mrs. Van Etten on how often the defendant came to her home. She couldn't say, but she had known him for thirty years and had been "friendly with him." When asked what they discussed during his visits, the witness responded that she "could not remember what he talked about at any time."

Following the testimony of the Van Ettens, District Attorney Stephan brought to the stand the senior Conine, Hiram, brother-in-law of the defendant. Described by the *Freeman* as "smiling, bald-headed, wearing a blue jumper and seeming to feel very happy," the elder Conine would testify that Van Gaasbeek had arrived at their home around ten o'clock on Monday evening. The defendant, according to Conine, "had a kind of a strange look on him—different from what I was used to seeing." Elaborating, he told the jury that he, too, believed Van Gaasbeek was drunk when he arrived at their house.

On cross-examination by Van Buren, the jury was given a rather detailed account of arrangements within the Conine home, a home that included the father, the three brothers and Emma Smith. Responding to a request by Van Buren to describe the sleeping arrangement within the household on the night Van Gaasbeek came by, Conine told the court that he had slept on a chair. Meanwhile, he continued, brothers George and Albert would take turns sleeping on a lounge while Arthur and Emma Smith, for the past year, had slept in the other room. On further questioning by Van Buren, however, Emma Smith's place within the Conine household and whom she was actually involved with grew unclear. It was, perhaps, a point Van Buren wanted exposed.

As Van Buren pressed Hiram Conine further, the witness contradicted himself, telling Van Buren that Arthur and Emma Smith had been sleeping in the other room for about three weeks—not the year he had previously stated. It was a contradiction that gave Van Buren an opportunity to explore the role of Emma on two levels. First, in an effort to shift the spotlight away from his client and undermine the testimony against him, Van Buren knew, in 1906 Ulster County, that any reference to a shared living arrangement between a black man and a white woman would unsettle most jurors. Second, and possibly more important, was the question as to whom, over time, Emma actually lived with, and if there had been a recent change in relationships within the Conine household. Such a change may indicate that all was not as presented within the Conine home.

> *Van Buren: "Where did she* [Emma] *live before she and Arthur took the back room?"*
> *Conine: "We all lived together."*
> *Van Buren: "Who had the woman?"*
> *Conine: "We all lived in one room."*
> *Van Buren: "Did she live with you as your wife?"*
> *Conine: "No."*
> *Van Buren: "Which of the boys did she live with?"*
> *Conine: "Arthur."*
> *Van Buren: "Before she took Arthur?"*
> *Conine: "She was with Arthur all the time."*

Though Van Buren sensed that Conine was not revealing the total truth about Emma Smith and past relationships within the family, he would, for the time being, move on. Wrapping up his questioning of Hiram, Van Buren transitioned to a different line of inquiry. Responding to a final question from Van Buren, the elder Conine told the jury that Oscar Harrison had been in his home on occasion. It was an admission that Van Buren, along with further questions regarding Emma Smith, would return to.

In his approach to the trial and in his efforts to convince the twelve white men occupying the jury box that Cornell Van Gaasbeek was an innocent man falsely accused, defense attorney Augustus Van Buren believed that the real truth in the case somehow connected itself to the Conine family. Adding to that belief would be his examination of Hiram's son, George Conine, as recorded by the *Kingston Daily Freeman*.

Approaching George Conine as he sat in the witness stand, Van Buren's opening would take the witness—and the courtroom—by surprise. Van Buren knew of the corncob pipe, along with some Mullen's tobacco (a local product out of Higginsville that the *Freeman* noted was "the product of every true and loyal son of Ulster County") that had been found at the scene. He also knew that Cornell Van Gaasbeek did not use Mullen's, let alone a corncob pipe.

> *Van Buren: "George, have you any smoking tobacco on you?"*
> *Conine: "Guess, I have."*
> *Van Buren: "Let me see it, will you? Mullen's isn't it?"*
> *Conine: "Yes sir, everyone smokes Mullen's up here."*
> *Van Buren: "Got your pipe with you?"*
> *Conine: "No sir."*
> *Van Buren: "Where's it at?"*
> *Conine: "I don't know."*
> *Van Buren "Lost it?"*
> *Conine: "Guess not."*
> *Van Buren: "When did you have it last?"*
> *Conine: "Today."*
> *Van Buren: "Where are you stopping in Kingston?"*
> *Conine: "With my brother."*
> *Van Buren: "Suppose you left it there?"*
> *Conine: "Don't know. Maybe."*
> *Van Buren: "Where did you buy it?"*
> *Conine: "Beekman's."* [Referring to the general merchandising store in Woodstock.]
> *Van Buren: "How much did you pay for it?"*
> *Conine: "Twelve cents."*
> *Van Buren: "Clay?"*
> *Conine: "I don't use clay."*

Van Buren: "What do you use?"
Conine: "Mostly corncob."

A bit puzzled by the line of questioning regarding Mullen's tobacco and what kind of pipe the witness used, the *Freeman* reporter doubted its effectiveness, stating, "The only defect in Mr. Van Buren's Mullen's theory is that there may be smokers of Mullen's on the jury, and no smoker of Mullen's can ever be brought to believe that any person who smokes 'the pride of Higginsville' could ever be guilty of a crime."

Having established that George Conine used a corncob pipe, Van Buren had other questions for the witness, a witness who, like his father, Van Buren fully suspected knew more than he was willing to admit. Specifically, the defense attorney began to zero in on the morning Van Gaasbeek and Conine discovered Harrison's body. Returning to testimony Conine had given earlier, Van Buren noted that Conine had not gone any farther than the front step of Van Gaasbeek's home. And yet, after the defendant had squeezed through the door to find the body of Harrison on the floor and called to Conine, "What shall I do?," Conine responded by telling him to call the dead man's father. There was just one problem with his suggestion. Conine had testified that he had seen only the leg and a foot of the dead man. As Van Buren pointed out to the jury, Van Gaasbeek "had not said who the body was."

Under further questioning by Van Buren, George Conine was asked, as his father had been, to describe to the jury living conditions within the two-room Conine household. Just prior to the day Oscar Harrison was murdered, Conine reiterated, the three brothers, their father and Emma Smith occupied the house. At this point, however, the younger Conine's testimony began to diverge from his father's. On the evening of Harrison's death, the elder Conine had testified, his son Arthur and Emma Smith occupied one room in the house, while he and his two sons stayed in the other. Only weeks before, however, Van Buren had learned that those living arrangements hadn't been as stable as the Connies had acknowledged. Pressing the younger Conine, Van Buren extracted what, in fact, was reality. Stating that his father and Emma Smith had actually "set-up housekeeping" earlier in the winter, George Conine contradicted his father's testimony when he revealed that "brother Arthur supplanted father about three weeks before the murder."

Finally, Van Buren went looking for motive and to cast further suspicion on the Conine household. The motive for Harrison's death, he seems to have believed, was somehow connected to the white woman, Emma Smith, who lived with the Conines and, Van Buren believed, may have also had a budding relationship with Harrison. Were he able to raise the slightest possibility that such a relationship might have existed, then, perhaps, jealousy as a motive could be laid at the doorstep of one of the Conines.

As Van Buren attempted to weave his way through testimony that he hoped would, again, expose to the jury a situation sorely lacking in accepted 1905 morality, he also managed to establish that Harrison was no stranger to the Conine household. With George Conine testifying that he had known Oscar Harrison "since he was a little boy," he also admitted that Harrison had taken food at their table. Van Buren's next question, seemingly innocent on the surface, was, in light of what had already been established, meant to imply more than the simple response it appeared to seek.

"Slept there?" asked Van Buren, referring to Harrison.

"O, yes," was the response.

To conclude the prosecution's case, District Attorney Stephan called would-be detective Everett Roosa to the stand for the primary purpose of reminding the jury that Van Gaasbeek had fled town following the discovery of Harrison's body on the floor of his home.

Recounting much of what had already been published regarding his pursuit of Van Gaasbeek through the mountains and into Greene County, Stephan concluded Roosa's testimony by asking him to recount the brief conversation he had had with Van Gaasbeek in Purling. Describing how he had returned to Purling to find Van Gaasbeek at the town's post office, Roosa, as reported by the *Freeman*, testified that he asked Van Gaasbeek, "What did you lay that fellow out that way for?" Van Gaasbeek, according to Roosa, hung his head and replied, "I don't know."

To support Roosa's retelling of "the chase" from Woodstock, over the mountain and ending in Purling, Stephan brought to the stand a witness with the most unique name encountered so far in the trial, Rasmus Rasmussen. Rasmussen, living in West Saugerties, testified that Van Gaasbeek had come to his home on Tuesday evening. Claiming he was on his way to Tannersville, the defendant inquired of Rasmussen if he might spend the night and escape the cold. Rasmussen agreed to let the stranger stay in his kitchen for the night, and with the arrival of morning, Van Gaasbeek, preparing to leave, inquired of his host if there was a charge for the evening. Being told that there was none, Cornell Van Gaasbeek offered his thanks and went on his way.

9
VAN GAASBEEK TAKES THE STAND

Though the hour on that Thursday afternoon grew late, it was time for Augustus Van Buren to offer a defense by putting his client before the jury. Prior to doing so, however, he addressed the twelve white men before him. Not quite secure how they might view the testimony of the defendant speaking to them from the witness stand, he reminded them that they were duty bound to listen to the testimony they were about to hear "without prejudice."

With his client sworn in and seated on the stand, Van Buren was in no hurry to explore the events surrounding Harrison's death. Rather, in an effort to personalize Van Gaasbeek's story, Van Buren took his client through a series of questions that revealed his basic life history, including employment. And, in the process, Van Buren hoped to establish his client as a religious person in the eyes of the jury.

Stating that he was fifty-four years old and would turn fifty-five on June 19 of that year, Van Gaasbeek told the court that he had been born in Woodstock, that his father had been deceased some twenty-eight years and that his mother had "been dead eight or nine years." From there, he began establishing that he had long been a hard worker, finding employment whenever and wherever he could. Citing work that he undertook, primarily in Kingston, Van Gaasbeek ticked off the various jobs he held, beginning with a position as coachman and gardener for Mrs. Cornelius Bruyn, a position he held for eight years and one that only terminated with his employer's death. He would go on to serve as a coachman yet again for a Mrs. Hester in Kingston, who, in 1903, was said to have purchased one of the finest teams of seal brown horses in Ulster County. Following a stint on an ice wagon for DeWitt Cunyes and F.S. Van Wagenen in Kingston, Van Gaasbeek sought work back in Woodstock, eventually catching on with a construction crew working the state road between Woodstock and Saugerties. Once that work was concluded, it became a matter of what odd jobs he could find around Woodstock.

As Van Buren began to approach his client's relationship with the younger Harrison, he did so in a way that he hoped would project positively on the jury. Asking Van Gaasbeek to tell jurors how long he had known Harrison and how they had come to meet each other, Van Gaasbeek responded that they had been friendly for three or four years and that he "used to come up to Woodstock to church and in that way I got acquainted with him."

Not minimizing his relationship with the victim, Van Gaasbeek also related that one Sunday, while he was next door at the Conine home, Harrison arrived there. Mentioning that he was out of work, Harrison said he would like to stay with Van Gaasbeek for a while. That night, Van Gaasbeek told the jury, they went to church.

While Harrison stayed with Van Gaasbeek for a couple of weeks, he eventually left and would not be seen by the defendant for almost a month. Presumably, this was the period of time when Harrison left Woodstock to join with the *Peck's Bad Boy* traveling show. It wasn't until the Saturday before his death that Harrison would again appear at Van Gaasbeek's house in Zena. Staying through the weekend, which included a rainy Sunday, Harrison was still there on Monday, according to Van Gaasbeek's testimony.

Admitting that Harrison had been at his home on the day prior to the discovery of his body, Van Gaasbeek testified that the two discussed where to find some work in town. Stating that he told Harrison he was going into Woodstock to speak to someone he had worked with about finding quarry work, Van Gaasbeek then testified that he left for Woodstock around five o'clock in the afternoon. As he left, the defendant recalled, Harrison was still at his house but said he was going over to the Conines for a bit before heading back to his parents' home. "That," said Van Gaasbeek, "was the last I saw him—when he went to Conines."

After leaving Harrison behind, the defendant recalled that, on arriving in Woodstock, he stopped in Beekman's general store before heading to Van Etten's. At Van Etten's, he talked to the husband about the possibility of finding work in one of the still-active quarries in Woodstock. Admitting that he stayed later than expected, Van Gaasbeek also admitted that he was a "little drunk" from drinking cider.

> *Van Buren: "Hard cider, I suppose?"*
> *Van Gaasbeek: "Not too hard. No sir."*

At this point, Van Buren began to lead his client through the events of Monday evening and into Tuesday morning. Explaining, according to the *Freeman*, that it was a very cold night and, having not been home since the afternoon, Van Gaasbeek told the court that "he hated to make a fire that time of night, so I walked into Conines, as I had done often before." The next morning as he prepared to go back to his house to make breakfast, he noticed that George Conine was out at the woodpile talking to Arthur. When George came back inside he told Van Gaasbeek, "Last night when I went out for a pail of water I heard a terrible noise over in your house. Maybe it was Oscar Harrison and there is something wrong with him."

Not sure what to make of George's comment, the defendant told the jury that he and George proceeded to make the short walk to his home. Pushing the door open, Van Gaasbeek saw the body of young Harrison lying on the floor. Panicked, agitated or nervous (take your pick), Van Gaasbeek yelled to George, "What can this mean? What shall I do?" It was at that point, without having been inside to actually see Harrison's face, that George, according to Van Gaasbeek, told him that he should telephone the boy's father.

From there, Van Gaasbeek recounted his two trips back and forth to the Wolven home asking for someone to contact Oscar's father. On his second visit, as Wolven telephoned Harrison again, Van Gaasbeek related to the jury that Wolven suggested, if it were him, that he would go off and fetch Doctor Downer. Van Gaasbeek, offering that he wasn't sure what to do, testified that he eventually took Wolven's advice and left to locate the Woodstock doctor.

As he set off to Woodstock, however, Van Gaasbeek went from someone intent on seeking help to someone realizing the gravity of the situation he was in and the questions that would likely follow. With a dead man lying on the floor of his house, he began to rationalize, he might be better off to simply make himself scarce.

He told the jury that while he originally set out to reach the doctor, he "just kept walking." In describing the so-called chase over the mountain, Van Gaasbeek offered by way of explanation, "I didn't know where I was going and I went on till I was arrested by this man Roosa."

Van Buren: "Why did you go?"
Van Gaasbeek: "Well, when I went in the house and found Harrison lying there I didn't know what to do or where I was going."
Van Buren: "You got scared and you went."
Van Gaasbeek: "Yes sir, that's it."

When asked directly by Van Buren if he had killed Harrison, Van Gaasbeek, according to the *Freeman*, "denied with emphasis" that he hadn't, exclaiming, "God knows I didn't."

The headline in the *Kingston Daily Freeman* that recounted Van Gaasbeek's testimony proclaimed the following: "Testimony of Van Gaasbeek—Defendant Made a Poor Witness in His Own Behalf."

The "poor witness" opinion seems to have flowed from the cross-examination by District Attorney Stephan, during which Van Gaasbeek became confused and seemed to contradict himself when it came to the state of his sobriety prior to Harrison's death. Asked to state where and when he had gotten his hard cider, Van Gaasbeek claimed to have gotten the first jug on the Friday prior to discovering the body. On further questioning, his story changed. Van Gaasbeek told Stephan that it was on Saturday and that Oscar Harrison had gotten the cider. The story seemed to change yet again when Van Gaasbeek stated that he had also gotten a second jug from a man named Charlie Cooper but that he "didn't drink any Sunday because it was all gone."

Since there had already been testimony by multiple witnesses that they had seen Van Gaasbeek intoxicated on Monday, District Attorney Stephan asked the witness where he had gotten the cider that specific day. Van Gaasbeek responded that he got it from the two jugs previously mentioned. Stephan reminded the witness that he had just testified that the jugs were empty by Sunday. Had "he filled them again?" Van Gaasbeek responded that he had not, offering that he wasn't sure if "they had been entirely empty."

Then, out of the blue, according to the published report, Stephan asked Van Gaasbeek if "he had ever struck and cut Floyd Elwyn with a knife or razor?"

While Van Gaasbeek was offering that he had "never been convicted," Van Buren quickly rose with an objection. "Sustained," declared Judge Cantine.

As the defense neared the end of its presentation, two of Van Buren's last witnesses, Charles Merrit and Thomas Johnston, were called to the stand to testify to Van Gaasbeek's character. Johnston, a police officer, told the jury that he had known the defendant for thirty years. Similarly, Merrit had known Van Gaasbeek for "25 or 30 years" and that, at one point, he had even employed the defendant. When Merritt was asked by Van Buren to testify regarding Van Gaasbeek's character and reputation, however, Judge Charles F. Cantine brought a halt to his line of questioning, ruling such questions out of order.

While Merritt was called to the stand by Van Buren as nothing more than a character witness, it is doubtful that anyone in the courtroom that day could have comprehended just how critical his testimony—or lack of it—would be to the future of Cornell Van Gaasbeek.

With that, the defense rested.

Prior to summations, the prosecution endeavored to tie up a loose end as well as make a further attempt to place Van Gaasbeek's past on the record. Calling George Conine back to the stand, Stephan asked the nephew if Harrison, as testified by the defendant, had come to their home on the day before his body was discovered. The answer was no. Had he told Van Gaasbeek that Harrison had been to their home that day? Again, the answer was no.

Finally, Stephan called City Recorder Harry Groves to the stand. Producing a record from an 1893 court docket, Groves offered that Van Gaasbeek had been convicted of a misdemeanor. Once again, Van Buren rose to object. Once again, Judge Cantine sustained the motion, and the testimony was not admitted.

With the last witnesses called, the trial turned to summations and to deliberation by the jury.

10
SUMMATIONS AND VERDICT

Friday morning, January 12, dawned fair with temperatures expected to reach a high of thirty-nine degrees. As the parties assembled before Judge Cantine that morning, summations would be the first order of business. For Frederick Stephan, the task was fairly straightforward. In a matter-of-fact way, taking his time so that the jury clearly grasped the importance of the testimony before them, Stephan highlighted the events and actions that, in his considered opinion, could lead to only one conclusion: guilty. While there was no direct, eyewitness testimony he could point to that would conclusively tie Van Gaasbeek to the murder of Harrison, certainly the preponderance of the circumstantial evidence presented—where Harrison's body was found, the testimony of the Conines relating to the sounds heard coming from Van Gaasbeek's cabin, the inconsistencies in the defendant's story, the intoxicated state many had seen him in and, ultimately, his decision to flee and escape the law that he knew would be coming for him—could lead to only one reasonable conclusion. As he hammered home each fact he wanted the jury to remember and consider, Stephan—piece by piece—built his case. And, as he concluded, he pointed in the direction of the only person those facts could implicate: Cornell Van Gaasbeek.

In contrast to Stephan, Augustus Van Buren went about his summation in a far different, more emotional manner as he attempted to demonstrate the lack of specific evidence against his client. Beginning with his belief that the prosecution had failed to offer a motive for the murder of Harrison and that the evidence presented was thinly circumstantial at best, Van Buren told the jury that while Van Gaasbeek "may" have killed Harrison, so it was equally possible that George or Arthur Conine "may" have perpetrated the brutal act. And, as summarized by the *Freeman*, Van Buren concluded, "Any of these things may have happened, but a jury cannot convict a man on what may have occurred."

Van Buren then proceeded to attack the testimony of Everett Roosa, "a gentleman," he offered, "on whom fame burst in a day—an obscure individual who leaped in an instant into an eternal fame." Not content with his initial portrayal of Roosa, Van Buren went further, characterizing him as "the most ridiculous man on earth" and as a "half-baked ignoramus." Continuing, Van Buren concluded with the thought that Roosa believed himself to be "Webster's dictionary and encyclopedia combined, and when he gets one idea in his cranium you cannot force another in without an explosion."

As he attacked the credibility of Roosa, Van Buren did so in an effort to convince the jury that simply because his client had run away was no reason to charge him with the crime of murder. In fact, he offered, you could equally argue that to remain in Woodstock might have been the "safest course," so as not to draw even more attention to himself.

Finally, surprising the jury and those gathered in the courtroom, Van Buren brought his summation to a close by raising the emotional tone of his discourse by telling of his relationship with Van Gaasbeek through the years. Noting that he and the defendant used to go swimming together as children, he described their relationship as not unlike a "parti-colored Damon and Pythias affair," citing the Greek myth that symbolizes the ideal friendship in which one is willing to give his life for the other. It was his final statement, however, that more realistically underscored the true nature of that relationship within the context of 1906. "Cornell Van Gaasbeek," Van Buren declared, "was a good natured ignorant fool of a nigger who wouldn't hurt a mosquito."

With summations concluded, Judge Cantine began his instructions to the jury at 12:15. Following a review covering the different degrees of murder and manslaughter, the jury was charged and asked to begin its deliberations.

At one 1:00 p.m., the jury left the courtroom, and, for all, the waiting began.

The wait would not be a long one. Having been dismissed at 1:00 p.m., the jury then took an hour for lunch. By 4:30 p.m. on that Friday, they let it be known that they had reached a verdict.

On entering the courtroom and taking their seats, as reported by the *Freeman*, the members of the jury were asked by the clerk, "Gentlemen of the jury have you agreed upon a verdict?"

> *"We have," replied the foreman, Stephen Warren, from the town of Ulster.*
> *"How say you? Do you find the defendant guilty or not guilty?"*
> *"Guilty," replied Warren.*
> *"Of the crime charged in the indictment?" asked the clerk.*
> *"Yes," replied Warren.*

At this point in the formal proceeding, however, the clerk committed a rather major error when stating the charge against Van Gaasbeek.

"Listen to your verdict as the court hath recorded," the clerk began. "You say you find the defendant guilty of the crime of murder in the second degree. So say you all?"

Confusion reigned for the moment. "No. Manslaughter in the first degree," juror John Shields interrupted. Foreman Warren concurred.

Stepping in, Judge Cantine polled each juror to ensure all were in agreement. With each name called, the answer was the same, "manslaughter in the first degree."

The correction was an important one when it came to the severity of the sentence that would be delivered. Murder in the second degree—the killing of a human with the intent to kill—carried a sentence of life. Manslaughter in the first degree—the killing of a person in the heat of passion, without the intent to kill—was punishable by a sentence not to exceed twenty years.

As it was, according to the *Freeman*'s own analysis, the twelve men of the jury had arrived at the belief that Van Gaasbeek had struck Harrison "while so drunk that he scarcely knew what he was doing."

Throughout the confusion, as others dictated and directed his fate, Van Gaasbeek was described as sitting "without any display of emotion."

Sketch of Cornell Van Gaasbeek as it appeared in the *Kingston Daily Freeman* during the trial. *Retrieved from digitized scan. HVRH website.*

11
AFTERMATH

Following the announcement of the verdict on Friday afternoon, Judge Cantine halted proceedings for the day and announced that sentence would be imposed on the following Monday. As a result, as Van Gaasbeek was left to ponder his fate over the weekend, word began to spread that the jury had delivered a verdict of guilty. So it was, when court reconvened on Monday afternoon and the doors to the courtroom were opened, those wishing to hear sentencing imposed, according to the *Freeman*, "were so numerous that they seemed to hang on the window sills and sides of the room like flies in August."

Monday's proceedings began with Van Buren making a motion for a new trial, a motion quickly denied by Cantine. District Attorney Stephan then moved for sentencing, at which point Judge Cantine began questioning Van Gaasbeek on some basic background questions:

> Cantine: "*Age?*"
> Van Gaasbeek: "*Fifty-five.*"
> Cantine: "*Employment?*"
> Van Gaasbeek: "*Laborer.*"
> Cantine: "*Education?*"
> Van Gaasbeek: "*Could read and write.*"
> Cantine: "*Religion?* "
> Van Gaasbeek: "*Received religious instruction in the Reformed Church.*"

Once Cantine concluded his questions of the now-convicted Van Gaasbeek, he turned directly to pronouncing sentence: seventeen years in prison, to be served at Dannemora Prison in Upstate New York.

With that, it was over. In a matter of six weeks, Cornell Van Gaasbeek had been arrested, tried and convicted, a process the *Kingston Daily Freeman* lauded in an editorial as "prompt and efficient." The *Freeman* would go on to praise the efforts of the district attorney's office, noting that while the case was, at first, slow to develop, once District Attorney Stephan became involved, a "prompt and thorough investigation" ensued, securing "the necessary evidence, much of which would have been obliterated had delay ensued."

In addition to the praise offered to the district attorney, the paper went on to laud the efforts of Everett Roosa, writing: "Although Roosa has read of the doings of Sherlock Holmes and Nick Carter, and believes there are valuable suggestions in the stories of these mythical detectives, he is no storybook detective himself. Hard common sense characterized his movements." As a result, "much of the credit for the conviction" is due to him.

Back in his cell in uptown Kingston, Van Gaasbeek waited. Soon they would come for him to begin the 262-mile journey upstate. At age fifty-five, with a seventeen-year sentence ahead of him, it was questionable, once he left Ulster County, if he would ever again see the only landscape he had ever known.

ONLY TWO DAYS AFTER Judge Cantine had sentenced Van Gaasbeek, racial conflict again found its way into local headlines. In a case involving an assault on a young black girl on her way home from a church lecture in Kingston, a white man standing outside a saloon, was accused of grabbing her arm and striking "her in the mouth until her lips bled and called her vile names."

Due to her age, the young girl was accompanied in court by her father, described by the *Freeman* as being "typical of the better class of jolly southern Negroes." Also appearing before the judge was the victim's brother, who had been with her on the night of the alleged assault. Testifying on behalf of his sister, the brother identified the assailant and offered, "Oh, I've heard of him before and what he does to colored men. I knew I wasn't man enough to tend to him and I run, I did....I got away as quick as I could and went up the street after a cop."

Later in his testimony, the brother stated that, after he and the police officer had followed the assailant and his friends and hid to surprise them, he overheard, as they approached, "Well, we will go back and clean up them niggers."

While the accused would argue that he only responded after he had been punched first, the incident, following so closely on the trial of Van Gaasbeek, could have only exasperated local racial tensions.

Testament to such tensions would come less than two weeks later, as the issue of "southern Negroes" coming north and competing for jobs in local brickyards came to the fore. With the headline, "Brickyard Laborers Draw Color Line," the *Freeman* reported that members of the International Brick, Tile and Terra Cotta Workers Alliance had arrived in the area to organize some six hundred local workers. Promising that the union would fight for higher wages, organizers also pledged that they would see to it that "no more southern Negroes" would be hired in the yards along the Hudson.

Cornell Van Gaasbeek, however, would know none of what was occurring in the city and the area he had always called home. He now sat in a different cell far to the north.

12

FAINT HOPE

With the nickname of "Little Siberia," due to its remoteness and brutal winters, what local papers referred to as "Dannemora" at the time of Van Gaasbeek's sentence was, officially, the Clinton Correctional Facility and had long stood as home to many of New York's most hardened criminals. First opened in 1844 as part of a legislative act establishing the prison "for the purpose of employing convicts in mining and the manufacturing of iron," the initial group of prisoners arrived upstate in 1845. Three decades later, with efforts at mining abandoned, the prison began a period of expansion during the latter half of the nineteenth century. Included within that expansion was the construction of more than six hundred additional cells. While, for a period of time, the prison would include serving prisoners diagnosed with tuberculosis, Clinton was also the site of New York's electric chair from 1895 to 1914. By the time Cornell Van Gaasbeek arrived upstate, Clinton was known to specialize in housing those prisoners considered "incorrigible" due to an 1897 classification of inmates by the number of offenses they had committed. As a result, "Clinton received the worst, those with three or more felony convictions."

Such was the reality Cornell Van Gaasbeek faced as he arrived upstate. Back home, few seemed to give his life or the trial further attention. Newspapers no longer carried his name. The Conines and Emma Smith faded back into obscurity, and little more was heard from Everett Roosa.

Woodstock was also moving on in 1906. With the decision by the Art Students League to begin hosting summer classes in Woodstock, an increasing number of young artists became a familiar site around town. Woodstock would celebrate the Fourth of July that year with music, speeches, a fair, a double-header baseball game and an evening of fireworks. Later that year, after a fire in town once again brought home the fear of losing the entire village of wooden structures to flames, villagers met to officially form the Woodstock Fire Department. And, mere miles away, work was underway on construction of the Ashokan Reservoir

And yet, as the pages turned on the lives of most, one man continued to press for justice on behalf of Van Gaasbeek: Augustus Van Buren.

Unfortunately, for the man behind bars, it would take more than a year before Van Buren's efforts would begin to bear fruit on behalf of his client. Having shed his position as corporation counsel for the City of Kingston at the start of the year, Van Buren had returned to his law practice full time and, though much would occupy his attention, his work on Van Gaasbeek's appeal was always front and center. As he examined his options on how to center his appeal of the case, Van Buren looked to Judge Cantine's ruling that had denied testimony relating to his client's character. Believing that such a focus would serve as his best argument, the "reformer" moved forward, knowing, should his assessment and strategy fail, his childhood swimming friend would, more than likely, spend his remaining years behind the walls of Little Siberia.

On March 13, 1907, writing the opinion for the state's Appellate Division of the Supreme Court, Justice John M. Kellogg delivered the answer.

From the outset, Kellogg, after describing the basic facts before the court, seemed to focus on Van Buren's primary contention regarding character and the decision to disallow the related testimony that both Charles Merrit and Thomas Johnston were prepared to give on behalf of the defendant.

Kellogg's decision began:

> *The crime was committed in the town of Woodstock, where the defendant was born. For the last five or six years before the trial he had lived in that town, but prior to that time he had resided for many years in the city of Kingston and was well known there.*
>
> *One Merritt, who resided in the city of Kingston, swore that he had known the defendant for twenty-five or thirty years; that defendant had worked on his farm for him, on and off, three or four or five years, whenever he wanted extra help; he was acquainted with the reputation and character of the defendant so far as relates to whether or not he is of a quiet and peaceable disposition or otherwise. To the question as to what his reputation*

> is, the objection that no proper foundation had been laid for the proof and that it was not a proper way to show character was sustained and the defendant excepted.
>
> A policeman of the city of Kingston for the last nineteen years had known the defendant for thirty years; knew him whenever he was in the city and knew his character as to being a peaceable and quiet man. To the question as to what the character is, the same objection was sustained and the defendant excepted.
>
> This evidence probably related to the reputation of the defendant at Kingston and not in the town of Woodstock. The remoteness of time and place might weaken the testimony, but the fact that the man by living at Kingston many years before and up to five or six years before the trial had established a reputation for peaceableness and quietness was some evidence that that character had continued, especially in the case of a man fifty-five years of age.

As Van Buren continued to read through the decision, no doubt his hopes began to rise. Further indications as to where Kellogg's opinion was heading were to come as he examined the circumstantial evidence offered against Van Gaasbeek and how the question of character might have shifted the weight of evidence in the jury's mind.

> This defendant was on trial for killing his best friend, and the principal evidence of his connection with the crime was the fact that the deceased had been at defendant's cabin for some days; that they were more or less drunk, and that the deceased was found dead in the cabin, with other circumstances connecting the defendant more or less with the offense. Nobody knows just what caused the act, but it may fairly be inferred to have been a brutal cold-blooded murder. The assailant left the deceased in an unconscious and dying condition, and he died several hours after. If the fifty-five years of life of the defendant had given him among the people who knew him best a reputation as a quiet and peaceable man it might, in the minds of the jury, have some bearing upon the question whether he was guilty of the brutal murder of his friend.

Finally, after wading through further discussion and precedent on how to weigh the issue of character in such cases, Van Buren reached the final sentences of the decision:

A man on trial for a crime may have many traits of character which he may not desire to discuss before the jury; but if there is a redeeming feature in his character and that feature points to the improbability of his having committed the crime it would seem that he is entitled to the benefit of the evidence. A bad character for truth and veracity, for morality, and in other respects, does not make the person burdened with it an outlaw, the people who know him best as to render it improbable that he would be guilty of the particular crime charged against him.

Evidence of good character may of itself create a reasonable doubt, when without it none would exist.

The conviction and judgment should be reversed and a new trial granted.

Not only had Van Buren won his victory, the decision by the Appellate Division was unanimous.

Unfortunately for Van Gaasbeek and Van Buren, the reality of a new trial would be delayed as District Attorney Frederick Stephan sought to appeal the appeal. As he had during Van Buren's successful appeal attempt, Attorney Howard Chipp would once again represent the district attorney's office. Chipp, no doubt well acquainted with Van Buren, equally rivaled his opponent in both popularity and work ethic. The successful

Kingston Academy. In addition to his other roles, Howard Chipp served as the academy's honorary president. *Author's collection.*

Attorney Howard Chipp. *Courtesy of the Ulster County Clerk's Office.*

lawyer served, in 1907, not only as president of the Ulster County Bar Association but also as a director for the Kingston Consolidated Railroad Company, as a trustee for the Ulster County Savings Company and as honorary president of Kingston Academy. And although Chipp seems to have been District Attorney Stephan's "go-to" counsel when it came to arguments before the Appellate Division, his second effort before the court ended the same as his first. Once again, Van Buren had argued that the prohibition against testimony attesting to his client's character had seriously jeopardized Van Gaasbeek's case. And, once again, Van Buren prevailed. It was a decision, according to the *Freeman*, "that will be read with interest by lawyers throughout the state."

13
THE FINAL BATTLE

With a new court date set, Cornell Van Gaasbeek returned to the all-too-familiar accommodations of an Ulster County jail cell to await his second chance. By this time on the calendar, spring had begun to show signs of overtaking winter. In late February, two days of rain on top of melting snow followed by freezing temperatures led to the main road into Woodstock being blocked by several feet of ice from an overflowing Sawkill. It would take thirty men working most of a day to finally blast and chop their way through the ice before the road could be reopened.

No doubt, after a day's work attempting to break through the ice, the workers might have appreciated a stiff and warming drink to ease the pain of their efforts. Unfortunately, those seeking such relief in Woodstock would find only disappointment. In the 1907 election, Woodstockers had voted for the town to go "dry," and, legally, the act of public consumption of alcohol was not an option before them.

On Monday March 16, 1908, more than two years after his conviction, Cornell Van Gaasbeek once again sat in a courtroom surrounded by a sea of white faces as a new jury was selected to hear his defense. Ironically, shortly before his trial opened, readers of the *Freeman* would be reminded that it had taken a civil war—concluded only forty years earlier and resulting in over 700,000 deaths—to free black men and women from bondage.

On Saturday, February 23, a reunion of veterans who had served in New York's 120th Regiment during the war was held in Kingston's Eagle Hotel, only a short walk from Van Gaasbeek's cell. Woodstock's last connection to

Ulster County jail and courthouse. *Courtesy Friends of Historic Kingston.*

the regiment, Aaron Risely, was unable to attend the reunion but took the time to send a note of regret to those gathering in Kingston:

> *I will not be able to meet with the boys this year. I have not been feeling good and have kept pretty close to the house this winter. I am sorry; I would have liked to be with you and shake hands with the boys. I think this is the first reunion I have been absent from on Washington's Birthday. You know the bear saw his shadow on the second of February, which was Candlemas Day; therefore he had to go back in his den for six weeks. It was a good thing he went back, or he would have frozen to death, as the thermometer was 28 below zero. I expect to stay in my den until the middle of March. Remember me to all the boys.*

Risely and the others of the 120th had offered their lives so that the burden of America's original sin could be lifted. How far the nation, including the North, had come since the days the 120th took to the field was about to be tested once again on a very local level.

As Cornell Van Gaasbeek looked around the courtroom that Monday morning, an unfamiliar face at the table for the prosecution glanced back at him. He would soon learn that the young face returning his gaze would have much to do with his future. In 1907, while Van Gaasbeek sat in Dannemora waiting for word on the success or failure of the appeal Van Buren had filed, William Cunningham had been elected district attorney in Ulster County. Easily outdistancing his Democratic rival, Cunningham, a Republican, was portrayed in the local press as a rising star within the county. Not quite thirty years old at the time of his election, the Ellenville native had already served in the New York State Assembly, where, according to the *Freeman*, "He has been generally recognized as one of the most efficient representatives the district has had in many years both in the energy he has displayed in the interests of his immediate constituents." With a background that included having worked his way through college and law school while receiving high honors, a stint with a prestigious law firm in New York City and an offer of a professorship at Kansas University, Cunningham would prove an interesting challenge to the seasoned Van Buren.

The second trial would begin at precisely eleven o'clock in the morning when a face quite familiar to Van Gaasbeek in the form of Judge Cantine took the bench. What would follow, however, was not what Cantine would have expected as, initially, confusion—and, to some extent, entertainment—became the order of the morning. To begin, of the three dozen potential jurors who had been called, only seven were present at the start of the session. Out of the seven who actually appeared, six of them requested that they be excused, three claiming they were hard of hearing. Because of the low turnout and the reluctance to serve by those who did appear, Van Buren and Cunningham found an early moment of agreement as Judge Cantine, hoping additional jurors would show, adjourned the session until later in the day.

When court reconvened that Monday, Judge Cantine would once again attempt to move toward the selection of a jury that, for a second time, would sit in judgment of Cornell Van Gaasbeek. Unfortunately for all involved, the process would not be much of an improvement over the morning session. Leading with the headline "Jurors' Answers Are Entertaining," the *Kingston Daily Freeman* went on to describe both the humor and the frustration the lawyers and Judge Cantine found as they proceeded through the afternoon hours.

One of the first jurors to actually undergo questioning—after Judge Cantine had already dismissed eight potential jurors due to "illness"—told the court that he should be excused because he didn't know anyone in Kingston. Obviously frustrated at this point and not wishing to hear any further excuses, Cantine simply told the man that the trial "would be an excellent opportunity to get acquainted, then." The judge's patience was

Early Racial Injustice in Upstate New York

William Cunningham who served as district attorney for the second trial. *Courtesy of the Ulster County Clerk's Office.*

tried even further when Albert Kubeck walked into court and told His Honor that he couldn't wait around too long because he had "too much business on hand." As he continued on, explaining that he was only there because he had been served with a subpoena, Judge Cantine interrupted him, making it clear that he didn't care to hear any more. Sending Kubeck back to his seat, Cantine only tried the man's impatience further by stating that he would hear what he had to say at a later point in the day.

Augustus Van Buren would have his own patience tested when it was his turn to question yet another potential juror, James O'Neil of Warwarsing. He told District Attorney Cunningham that he had heard of the case against Van Gaasbeek, but he didn't really know the details. He further offered to Cunningham that he had "no prejudice against Negroes."

Van Buren would begin his questioning of O'Neil by asking him if he knew the district attorney.

> O'Neil: "I do and I don't. I know of him but not to speak to. He's a politician, isn't he?"
> Van Buren [unable to resist]: "Kind of one."
> O'Neil: "I voted for him."
> Van Buren: "Suppose the evidence was evenly balanced, what would you do?"
> O'Neil: "I'd speak out. There's one of two questions to answer, is he innocent or guilty? He must be one or the other."
> Van Buren: "Suppose there was doubt as to his innocence or guilt?"
> O'Neil: "I've heard there was such cases."
> Van Buren: "What would you do in such a case?"
> O'Neil: "I'd keep quiet."
> Van Buren: "You'd have to vote one way or the other. What would you do?"
> O'Neil: "I'd vote according to my mind."
> Van Buren [again]: "What would you do in such a case?"
> O'Neil: "I'd keep quiet."
> Van Buren: "You'd have to do something."
> O'Neil: "I don't know what I'd do. There's two sides to this; a man's life is worth something."
> Van Buren: "You're excused."
> O'Neil: "I'm glad of it."

Van Buren would challenge yet another potential juror when it seemed apparent that the man had already formed an opinion of guilt based on the evidence presented during Van Gaasbeek's first trial. Though George Cole told Van Buren that he would consider the arguments on both sides equally, Van Buren was not satisfied that the Kingston resident hadn't already arrived at a conclusion.

> Van Buren: *"You have formed an opinion?"*
> Cole: *"If them evidence was true, I formed an opinion, but I don't say them evidence was true. If them evidence was true, I have an opinion now and it would take evidence to remove it."*

As the questioning of jurors moved forward during the afternoon, two basic questions were once again of concern to the lawyers involved. Each juror addressed by Van Buren seems to have been questioned on their ability to dismiss prejudice during the course of the trial and during deliberations. William Swart of Saugerties offered that he had "no prejudice against Negroes." Stephen Roach of Shawangunk answered the same, as did Ira Palen of Marbletown, Ed Crispell of Olive and James White of Warwarsing. In fact, all potential jurors, according to press reports, indicated that the color of the defendant's skin would not be a factor in their decisions. Whether or not Van Buren believed them all is doubtful, as he issued multiple challenges during the afternoon.

Once again, for the prosecution, the question of circumstantial evidence rose as a point of concern. Issac Baird, also of Warwarsing, told the court that he had problems when it came to convicting on circumstantial evidence alone. Baird told Cunningham that the evidence would have to be "very strong" before he could find a man guilty based solely on circumstantial evidence. Baird was peremptorily challenged.

Of a similar opinion was Kingstonian Charles Koehler, telling the court that he believed in the need for direct evidence before he could find a person guilty. In Koehler's case, however, his problem with circumstantial evidence came not during questioning by District Attorney Cunningham but during questions posed by Van Buren. According to the *Freeman*, "Van Buren used the old illustration of two men being in one room, a pistol shot is heard, one cries out, 'You've shot me.' The other runs out of the room carrying a still smoking revolver in his hand and the first is found dead with a bullet in his heart."

> Van Buren: *"What would you do?"*
> Koehler: *"Find him not guilty, because nobody saw him do the shooting."*

Koehler was then challenged by Cunningham and dismissed by Judge Cantine.

Ultimately, despite some of the detours jury selection had taken, twelve white men were finally selected and sworn in to sit in judgment of Van Gaasbeek. As the lawyers involved in the case began to ready their arguments and call their witnesses, however, there were some noted and publicly announced changes that had occurred since the end of the first trial. In fact, as more than two years had passed since Van Gaasbeek had been found guilty, it was the very passage of time that may have most enhanced his chances for acquittal. For, over that period, two events had occurred that made their way into the public's knowledge about the case.

First, in a story of interest to all involved in the second trial, as well as providing a continued element of racial scandal that had surrounded the first trial, it was reported that Arthur Conine and Emma Smith had separated, or, as the *Kingston Daily Freeman* headline offered, "Witnesses in the Van Gaasbeek Case Are No Longer Affinities." The paper would continue by reporting that, although Arthur possessed "charms" that "particularly attracted Emma Smith, the white woman," the two had gone their separate ways and did not sit together in court and that "there was nothing to indicate the once friendly relations that existed between them." The *Freeman* would later report that following separating with Arthur, "the Smith woman is now living with another Negro."

Second, in August 1907, a story appearing in the same paper would bring a cloud of doubt and uncertainty to those who steadfastly pointed their finger at Van Gaasbeek as a murderer. In the time between Van Gaasbeek's first trial and the beginning of the second, two of the Conines—the father, Hiram, and his son, George—had died. Following their deaths, rumors began to circulate that one of them had "made a deathbed confession" to a local clergyman that he was responsible for young Harrison's death. The only problem with the rumor was that no one could assign any hard truth to a supposed confession. It was reported that county investigators—as well as Van Buren—were aware of the alleged confession but neither had been able to verify it. The *Freeman* had also launched an investigation, interviewing a number of local clergymen. They too came up empty in their pursuit, unable to find "any clergyman who would admit" to having received a confession from either Conine. And yet, unsubstantiated as the rumors were, published press reports regarding an end-of-life confession by one of the Conines certainly could not have been detrimental to Van Gaasbeek's chances going forward.

Still, as District Attorney Cunningham began to present his case, whatever rumors or "gossipy" news may have occurred prior to Van Gaasbeek's second trial, Augustus Van Buren knew that he would need more than rumors and gossip to prevent a return to Dannemora for his client

As Cunningham reminded the jury about the seriousness of the crime and offered that he would prove Cornell Van Gaasbeek was, beyond a reasonable doubt, guilty of taking the life of Oscar Harrison by violent means, many of the same witnesses from the first trial waited in the wings. First called was Charles Wolven, who, once again, recounted Van Gaasbeek's early-morning arrival at his home asking that he call Harrison's father and tell him that his son lay dead in his house. Wolven went on to describe going to Van Gaasbeek's house with Dr. Downer to find Oscar Harrison lying on his back with "one hand under his back and one along his side with fingers clenched. There was froth coming from his mouth: there was a bruise on his nose and on the cheek that looked like a blow had been struck."

After describing the scene further, including the hammer believed to have been the murder weapon and adding that there was blood on the victim's head, Wolven was turned over to the defense for questioning. Van Buren began with an attempt to have Wolven offer his assessment of Van Gaasbeek's character. No sooner had he asked the witness "What kind of fellow was he?" than objection was heard. This time, Judge Cantine, though sustaining the objection, noted that there would be time to establish character and reputation later. Van Buren moved on.

Asking Wolven to further describe how Van Gaasbeek appeared when he came to his house that morning, Wolven responded, according to the *Freeman*: "When Van Gaasbeek came to my barn he was so scared he trembled: he was a pretty scared nigger: I don't know whether he had been drinking. I think he said Oscar had poisoned or killed himself."

> *Van Buren: "Is that all Corney told you?"*
> *Wolven: "I can't remember all of it. I have other things to think about when I'm up home."*

Further testimony from Wolven once again took the jury through what he had observed while at Van Gaasbeek's house. After noting that Harrison "had on a jumper and overalls" and that "his coat was hanging from a peg in the wall," Van Buren asked about Wolven's actions later that day. Wolven went on to describe how he had joined Under Sheriff Webster in the search for Van Gaasbeek, a search that would eventually lead them to the Klondyke.

As owned by the Van Ettens, the Klondyke would not have been the type of place a respected member of the community such as the witness would have a high regard for. Sensing this, but also sensing that Wolven cared little to further engage in a discussion on how he viewed the Klondyke and its patrons, Van Buren, nonetheless, pressed on.

> *Van Buren: "What is the Klondyke?"*
> *Wolven: "I'd better leave that to you."*
> *Van Buren: "What kind of place is it?"*
> *Wolven: "I guess you better answer that…white people lived at the Klondyke."*
> *Van Buren: "About the same class as the colored people around here?"*
> *Wolven: "I'll leave that with you."*

Court was adjourned for the day.

The following morning, as court reconvened, familiar testimony from the first trial was offered by a host of witnesses. John Harrison, father of Oscar Harrison, recounted receiving the phone call from Charles Wolven telling him that his son was dead and had been found in the home of Van Gaasbeek. Wolven's wife, Carrie, confirmed her husband's testimony that a frightened Van Gaasbeek had arrived at their home asking that a call be placed to the senior Harrison. The morning session concluded with Dr. Henry Hoevenberg once again going over the autopsy he had performed on Harrison in the basement of the Reformed Church in Woodstock.

As a follow-up to Dr. Hoevenberg's testimony, the afternoon session on Wednesday began with Doctor Downer being called to the stand. Describing a morning phone call he had received from the elder Harrison, Downer testified that Harrison told him that he had received word that his son "had poisoned himself, or at any rate, was dead in a darkey's house" and asked if he would go there. Responding to further questions from District Attorney Cunningham, Downer presented specific testimony describing the scene he found on arriving at Van Gaasbeek's house. Offering that Harrison's face was covered with blood, he told the jury that he noticed a hammer lying on a nearby sofa. The face of the hammer, he testified, had blood on it and "two hairs were hanging to it." He also went on to describe, as others had before him, the disorder he found in Van Gaasbeek's house, disorder, he believed, that resulted from a fight. Finally, Downer, referring back to the autopsy conducted on Harrison, offered the opinion that the victim's death was caused "by blood clots on the brain and tearing of the brain tissue."

Downer's testimony regarding the autopsy would lead Van Buren, as he had in the first trial, to once again raise the question about Downer's "expertise" when it came to fractured skulls. Again Downer repeated that Harrison's was the fifth such injury he had witnessed and went on to review each case he had encountered. As the doctor concluded his answer, unlike the first trial, Van Buren restrained himself from again offering that "Woodstock must be a great place for broken skulls."

Leaving behind further discussion pertaining to Harrison's injuries, Van Buren went on to press Downer about the so-called disorder he claimed to have witnessed as the result of a fight inside Van Gaasbeek's home.

Van Buren: "Now let your imagination run riot, and figure out how much space was taken up by furniture and the body, and tell me how much floor space was not taken up by anything except floor covering?"
Downer: "About one hundred square feet."
Van Buren: "And the stove was there?"
Downer: "Yes."
Van Buren: "And the stand?"
Downer: "Yes."
Van Buren: "And the lamp on the stand?"
Downer: "Yes."
Van Buren: "And the chimney was on the lamp?"
Downer: "Yes."
Van Buren: "And a pair of spectacles on the stand?"
Downer: "Yes."
Van Buren: "And the dishes on the table?
Downer: "Yes."
Van Buren: [Somewhat incredulously, no doubt, as much seemed to have remained intact.] "And it looked as if there had been a struggle?"
Downer: "Yes."

Finally, Van Buren asked how long he had known the defendant. Responding that he had known Van Gaasbeek for "ten years," Van Buren followed with, "What did he do?"

Downer: "I don't know. I never saw him do anything."

When asked if he knew if the younger Harrison drank, Downer replied in the negative.

When Downer was dismissed, both lawyers conferred with Judge Cantine regarding the testimony George Conine had given at the first trial. Since

Conine had died prior to their current deliberations, how would his testimony be handled? Following discussion, it was determined that District Attorney Cunningham would read Conine's original testimony to the jury as he had responded to questions from the prosecution. Following that, Van Buren would read Conine's response to questions the defense had asked at the first trial.

So it was that, for the next hour, the jury listened as both lawyers read to them. Cunningham went over the key points Conine had offered to the first jury by describing how, having gone outside to the brush pile on the night in question, he heard "a groaning noise and stamping on the floor" coming from Van Gaasbeek's house. Later, he described how Van Gaasbeek had come into the Conine home a few hours later and "warmed his hands, sat down and went to sleep."

The following morning, Conine's testimony continued. He asked Van Gaasbeek about the noise he had heard the night before. Claiming he was afraid to go back to his house because of what Conine had told him, Van Gaasbeek asked Conine to come with him. Reaching Van Gaasbeek's house, Conine stated how the defendant had gone inside and yelled out, "Here he is, he is dead, look here."

Noticing only the left leg as he looked in, Conine had testified that he turned and started to return home, only to have Van Gaasbeek yell after him, "What shall I do?" At that point, Conine had stated that he told Van Gaasbeek to call the victim's father.

Making note that even though the defendant's nephew had told him to call the victim's father—even though Harrison's name had not been mentioned—Van Buren returned to the question of tobacco and the corncob pipe found in Van Gaasbeek's house. Van Buren slowly took the jury through that testimony in which George Conine stated he smoked Mullen's tobacco and used a corncob pipe. Knowing that his client did not use a corncob pipe, Van Buren had asked if Conine had his pipe with him. He did not. Nor could he account for its whereabouts.

Following the reading of Conine's testimony, yet another Conine, Albert, was called to the stand. Described by the *Freeman* reporter as "a short, very black Negro," Albert Conine testified in response to questions from the prosecution that the defendant did indeed come into their house very late on that Monday night and that his brother George had come in earlier. When Albert left the next morning, he told the jury, Van Gaasbeek was still there.

On cross-examination, Van Buren established through Albert's testimony that it was not unusual for Van Gaasbeek to sleep at the Conine home. In fact, he had done so "quite often." More importantly, in response to further questioning from Van Buren, Albert Conine told the jury that "the first he heard his brother George say anything about hearing the noise in Van Gaasbeek's house the time he went to the brush heap was at the courthouse on the first trial" and that he "never recollected hearing George and Arthur talk about the noise George said he heard."

Although the trial had moved quickly, as much of the testimony was an echo of the first trial, interest in the case had continued to build throughout the week. On Thursday, however, what had been a fairly crowded courtroom earlier in the week now spilled into the hallway. Part of the reason for the increase in attendance was the anticipated testimony of Cornell Van Gaasbeek. Additionally, those attending also knew that if Van Gaasbeek was on the stand, the trial was nearing an end and there was a good chance they could be present for the final summations.

Before those gathered would hear from Van Gaasbeek, however, two final witnesses for the prosecution would take the stand. The first to appear was Ida Van Etten, co-owner of the infamous Klondyke. Van Etten reiterated her testimony from the first trial, telling the jury that Van Gaasbeek was drunk when he came to her home on the night of the murder. Stating that he was nervous during his visit and that he staggered at times, Van Etten also told the jury that Van Gaasbeek mentioned a number of times that "he dreaded" going home.

The next witness to be called was none other than the self-proclaimed Sherlock Holmes devotee, Everett Roosa. With the fact that Van Gaasbeek had fled instrumental to the circumstantial case Cunningham was attempting to put before the jury, the tale of the chase conducted by Roosa from one county to the next was a key element for the prosecution. As Roosa took the jury through his pursuit of Van Gaasbeek, he related the words he and Van Gaasbeek shared once Roosa caught up with his quarry in the Greene County town of Purling.

> *Cunningham: "What did you say to him?"*
> *Roosa: "I said, 'Hello Corn' and he said 'hello.'"*
> *Cunningham: "Did you say anything else?"*
> *Roosa: "I said, 'I guess you'll have to come with me.' He said, 'What for?' I said, 'I guess you know. You'll have to go back and answer for that body lying in your home.' He got up and went out and got into the wagon. We drove to Jennings Hotel. In the washroom I said to him, 'You led me on a merry chase, Corn.' He said, 'I didn't think I'd get as far as I did.' 'What did you lay him out for?' I said. He hung his head and said, 'I don't know.'"*

For the moment at least, it seems that Van Buren was content with letting the testimony of both Van Etten and Roosa stand as delivered. The fact that there was no cross-examination, however, did not mean he would not challenge the implications their testimony carried at a later point.

With Roosa's testimony concluded, District Attorney Cunningham informed Judge Cantine that the prosecution rested. Rising from his seat at the defense table, Augustus Van Buren called his client to the stand.

While the press had reported during the first trial that Van Gaasbeek had not necessarily been the most effective witness on his own behalf, it appears, from a *Freeman* report on his testimony at his second trial, that the defendant was far better prepared.

Carefully led by Van Buren, Van Gaasbeek tended to remain close to basic facts as a means of rebutting previous testimony. Telling the jury that it was not uncommon for him to eat or sleep at the Conines', Van Gaasbeek stated, in fact, that he did so "oftener than he did at home." As for Oscar Harrison, the defendant explained that he had known the victim for "three or four years," that they were "friendly" and that they both "drank and got intoxicated."

At this point in the testimony, Van Buren asked Van Gaasbeek to take the jury through exactly what happened from the time Harrison first arrived at his home on the weekend before his death until he last saw him that Monday.

> *Van Gaasbeek: "Well, I think that Harrison came to my house on Saturday night, maybe 9 o'clock. He stayed there that night and Sunday and Monday till about half-past 2 or 3 o'clock. We talked Saturday night and drank a jug of cider. Sunday it rained and we stayed in the house all day except to go to Conine's to see what time it was. Harrison was with me Monday afternoon up to about 3 o'clock. We left side by side. I left him at Conine's. He said he was going home and what became of him after that I don't know. I didn't see him till the next morning at 7 o'clock, when George Conine called my attention to his body."*

Van Buren, citing the testimony given previously by Ida Van Etten, then asked Van Gaasbeek what he meant when he told her that "he dreaded" going home. Responding, Van Gaasbeek told the jury that he was referring to the fact that it was a bitterly cold night and that it was a two-mile walk to his house. He also noted that, upon arriving home, he went "directly" to the Conine house "because the fire in his house was out and it was cold."

After taking his client through a description of finding Harrison's body the next morning, Van Buren had Van Gaasbeek describe his state of mind at that point. Telling the jury that George Conine had told him he should call the father, Van Gaasbeek continued, "After that I didn't know what I was doing to tell the truth—leaving the man in health to meet him that way made me think—I don't know what."

Using that point in the retelling of events in the defendant's own words, Van Buren asked Van Gaasbeek about his encounter with Everett Roosa and the few words they exchanged in Pauling. Van Gaasbeek's response turned on interpretation, stating that he "understood Roosa to ask him what he knew about Harrison's death," to which he answered, "I don't know."

Finally, standing directly before his client, Van Buren asked, "Did you kill him?"

> *Van Gaasbeek: "No, Sir."*
> *Van Buren: "Did you strike him?"*
> *Van Gaasbeek: "No, Sir."*
> *Van Buren: "Did you ever have any trouble with him?"*
> *Van Gaasbeek: "Never had no trouble of no kind, never even had a sharp word. I think if I'd stayed there I would not have had all this trouble."*
> *Van Buren: "You surely wouldn't, that's for dead sure."*

On cross-examination, described by the *Freeman* as "searching," District Attorney Cunningham probed certain areas that appeared to conflict with the defendant's testimony at his first trial. Van Gaasbeek, however, stayed close to the story he had just told. When a discrepancy was pointed out, Van Gaasbeek would reply, according to the *Freeman*, "Yes, that's about the same thing," or, because of his state of mind at the time, "he didn't know what he was doing." When Cunningham returned to questions raised at the first trial regarding the number of jugs of cider that were consumed and where they had come from, Van Gaasbeek put forward a less confusing response, stating that Harrison had brought a gallon jug to his house and that he—Van Gaasbeek—also had a jug. He further told the court that, "I drank out of his jug and he drank out o' mine."

Seemingly unable to get Van Gaasbeek to repeat the confusing testimony he had offered at his first trial, Cunningham concluded his cross-examination.

For the most part, Cornell Van Gaasbeek's second trial had moved along much as the first. There were no great variations from the original testimony save for the fact that the defendant seemed to perform far better than he had almost two years earlier.

That was about to change.

Based on the appeal Van Buren had won, which led to the ruling that Van Gaasbeek was entitled to a new trial, the defense now called witnesses who would attest to the character of Cornell Van Gaasbeek. To that end, Van Buren called no less than five witnesses to the stand. They included Woodstock constable Thomas Johnson, James Winne, Frederick Van Wagonen, Charles Shufeldt and Adelbert Cooper. All of the witnesses called had known the defendant from between fifteen and thirty years and, under questioning by Van Buren, attested that, "drunk or sober," Van Gaasbeek's "reputation for peacefulness was good." Officer Johnson even managed to turn what most would fail to consider a ringing endorsement into high praise when he told the jury that even when he found Van Gaasbeek "asleep in a doorway and leaning against buildings," he always "went on about his business."

While Van Buren was finally able to put on the record testimony reflecting his client's character, he wasn't done in his efforts to plant the seeds for reasonable doubt in the minds of the jurors. Rather than resting his case at this point, Van Buren called two final witnesses to the stand who had not appeared at the first trial. Under the defense council's questioning, both Dr. George Chandler and Dr. Mark O'Meara testified, according to the *Freeman*, that "the contusions on Harrison's face and the fractures of his skull could have been caused by falling during an alcoholic fit." Both would also agree that "one fall would have been sufficient to cause all the wounds."

District Attorney Cunningham was quick to challenge such assertions by the witnesses. And, while Dr. O'Meara would, under questioning by Cunningham, continue to offer that it was indeed possible for Harrison's wounds to have been caused by a fall, he would retreat slightly and state that it may not have been "probable."

At that point in the day's proceedings, Judge Cantine adjourned court for the day. And yet, as those in attendance filed out of the courthouse onto Kingston's Wall Street that Thursday afternoon, Cunningham was not content to let the testimony of Van Buren's last two witnesses stand. As a result, he returned Friday morning with one last attempt to remove from the jurors' minds the possibility that Harrison had simply fallen while in a drunken stupor.

Friday, March 20, dawned fair and chilly. The temperature the night before had dipped into the twenties as winter had yet to release its grip on

Kingston's Wall Street. *Author's collection.*

the area. Knowing that the trial was nearing a climax, visitors once again crowded into whatever space they could find in the courtroom. At precisely 9:30 a.m., Judge Cantine called the court into session. As he did, District Attorney Cunningham rose to recall Dr. Van Hoevenberg to the stand in an effort to refute the testimony of the two doctors who had appeared the previous day on behalf of Van Gaasbeek. On hearing the prosecution ask Van Hoevenberg his opinion of the testimony offered by both O'Meara and Chandler the day before, Van Buren immediately rose to object that the question was improper. Judge Cantine sustained the objection, and the People rested once again.

With testimony finally concluded, Van Buren stood again to ask that Cantine direct the jury to "render a verdict of not guilty," arguing that the prosecution had failed to show that Harrison's death was "caused by a criminal agency." When his motion was denied, Van Buren then challenged that "criminal agency was not proven by a reasonable doubt; that it was not proved to a certainty; and that it was not proved that the defendant committed the act charged." Again, Judge Cantine denied Van Buren's request.

With motions concluded and a summation offered by the prosecution that, again, drew heavily on a preponderance of circumstantial evidence,

Augustus Van Buren rose for a final time, turned to the jury and began his own summation. It would become a summation that the *Freeman* reporter in the courtroom that day would call "Masterful."

Van Buren began by arguing that the prosecution had failed to simply provide a motive in their case against his client. In doing so, he also offered, somewhat surprisingly at first, that the propositions brought forth by the witnesses for the People were, "absolutely and unqualifiedly true." However, he would go on to argue, each "were susceptible of either an innocent or criminal interpretation," and, in that respect, "if a fact in the case will bear equally on two interpretations, that they—the jurors—must place the innocent interpretation or the innocent construction upon it."

But Van Buren had not come that day to simply argue law before the assembled jurors. Instead, he turned his summation in a more personal direction—a direction aimed at reaching the twelve men before him on a more human level, a level that would demonstrate his firm believe in his client's innocence.

"I know," pointing at Van Gaasbeek,

> *that all the criminal actions here alleged are foreign to the nature of this man. I knew him as a boy. I've grown up with him in a sense. And I have fought the fight of this Negro because I believe he is innocent and I'll fight it as long as there's any fight left in me. I played with him as a boy. We use to chase each other over the lowlands here in our boyish games and I want to say to you men that I believe that he would not wring the neck of a cat. I don't care what you do. I've dragged this case through every court in the state and I'll do it again if it's necessary and I don't care if it doesn't cost the County of Ulster a cent or if it bankrupts it. I am not a great believer in the law. I believe that nine times out of ten it's wrong. But I believe in eternal justice. I believe that if you can get a case away from the lawyers and into the hands of twelve honest, decent men you'll get justice and that is all I ask of you.*

As Van Buren concluded, he turned to find his client in tears, wiping his eyes with his handkerchief.

While the courtroom air hung heavy and quiet for a moment, Judge Cantine immediately turned to instructing the jury. Telling them that they were to entertain "no prejudices against circumstantial evidence, he further instructed the jury to decide whether or not they believed the witnesses and then draw inferences as they would from ordinary life." With possible consideration for Van Buren's last witnesses, Cantine also told the jury that "the first point to be decided is whether the injuries were self-inflicted. If the decision is that they were, you are to return to the courtroom." However, he continued, "if you decide that they were not self-inflicted, then you must decide the question: Was the death of Oscar Harrison caused by the criminal act of Cornell Van Gaasbeek?" Finally, according to press coverage, he instructed, "If you have reasonable doubt, under the evidence, as to whether these injuries were self-inflicted, you must find for the defendant."

With that, it was over. It had been 836 days since the discovery of Oscar Harrison's body, and the second trial of Cornell Van Gaasbeek had come to an end at 1:10 p.m. on a Friday afternoon in March 1908.

As the jurors filed out to begin their deliberations, many of the visitors to the courtroom that day, perhaps expecting a quick verdict, lingered. This time, however, a quick decision by the jurors would not be the case. As the twelve men deliberated into the evening, no unanimous verdict could be reached. And while some visitors remained until eleven o'clock that evening, it was finally announced that no decision would be forthcoming and that the jury had been sequestered for the night.

14

THE JOURNEY ENDS

As the jury worked its way through Friday evening debating the fate of Cornell Van Gaasbeek, Judge Cantine and District Attorney Cunningham spent their evening a short distance away at Kingston's Eagle Hotel. There, as members of the Ulster County Republican Club, the two joined a crowd of more than three hundred people welcoming and toasting the praises of New York's governor, Charles Evans Hughes. The future Supreme Court justice, presidential candidate and chief justice of the Supreme Court had arrived in Kingston along with his wife to both solidify local political support and rail against recent legislative proposals to introduce gambling in the state. It was an evening at which both Cantine and Cunningham had front-row seats, as dinner found them seated at "Table A" along with the governor, Congressman George Fairchild and other dignitaries. As they dined, as chronicled by the *Freeman*, on caviar, shad and filet mignon, perhaps they even acknowledged the presence at "Table C" of Woodstock supervisor Vactor Shultis and John Harrison's Woodstock friend, William Reynolds.

Meanwhile, as the evening slid into the early-morning hours, Cornell Van Gaasbeek waited. Unaware of the twists and turns his fate had taken during deliberations early that evening, the defendant slipped in and out of a fitful sleep.

Once gathered in the jury room, having been charged by Judge Cantine, the jurors had taken an initial vote to see where they stood. Their first ballot showed them deadlocked, six to six. As they deliberated into the evening, a second vote was taken. For the first time, Cornell Van Gaasbeek's future turned in a positive direction. The tally was nine for acquittal and three for conviction. Late in the evening, as the long day began to wear on their efforts, two more jurors moved into the not guilty column. Unable to declare themselves unanimous, however, the twelve men announced they were done for the evening.

Saturday morning, once again, dawned clear and fair. Temperatures, in fact, were expected to climb into the high thirties that day. As jurors reassembled over breakfast, their discussions continued. At some point during those early-morning deliberations, the final juror moved to join the others and declare Cornell Van Gaasbeek not guilty. At last, they were unanimous.

After more than two years of proclaiming his innocence—while so many had pointed the finger of guilt in his direction—the long ordeal of Cornell Van Gaasbeek was about to come to an end.

Judge Cantine brought the court into session at eight o'clock on Saturday morning, March 21, 1908. Oddly, while so many had waited the previous day for the jurors to return with a verdict, the courtroom, due to the early timing of the announcement, was empty of spectators. Only minutes after the judge entered the courtroom, the jury foreman stood and announced the verdict: "Not guilty."

Augustus Van Buren rose to thank the court, the jury and the district attorney "for the impartial manner in which the trial had been conducted from its inception to its close." Similarly, Judge Cantine both thanked and discharged the jury with a suggestion that "they get some sleep." As the principles began to file out of the courtroom, Cornell Van Gaasbeek insisted on shaking hands with each of the jurors, thanking them for their decision.

Only fifteen minutes after court had begun, Van Gaasbeek was back in his cell to collect what few belongings he had. At 8:20 that morning, he walked down the steps of the courthouse with his attorney and onto Kingston's Wall Street. For the first time since December 1905, he was a free man.

15
MOVING ON

It had been two years and four months since Cornell Van Gaasbeek first pounded on Charles Wolven's door and set in motion a process that would shock a small town and intertwine so many lives. For many of the individuals involved, it was finally time to move on.

And so they did.

Frederick Stephan, district attorney for the first trial

Following his three years as district attorney for Ulster County, Frederick Stephan would go on to serve two terms as a judge overseeing Kingston's city court. In addition to service for the Ulster County Board of Elections, Stephan enjoyed a forty-five-year career as a well-respected attorney in the area. Stephan suffered a stroke in September 1944 while shopping in Johnson's drugstore on the Strand in Kingston. He is buried in Kingston's Wiltwyck Cemetery alongside his wife, the former Alice Vignes.

WILLIAM CUNNINGHAM, DISTRICT ATTORNEY FOR THE SECOND TRIAL

In an ironic twist of fate, William Cunningham, after being nominated for another term as district attorney in 1910, went on to defeat Augustus Van Buren's son Alfred in the general election. In 1912, he ran statewide as the Republican candidate for comptroller. While outpolling all other candidates on the Republican ticket that year, he was defeated in an election that went heavily Democratic by almost 200,000 votes statewide. In yet another attempt at a statewide office, Cunningham was turned back in the Republican primary for secretary of state in 1914. In 1915, Cunningham was elected secretary of the state's Constitutional Convention and, also in 1915, was appointed judge of the court of claims and served until 1922. Cunningham died in 1943 and is buried in the Fantinekill Cemetery in Ellenville.

JUDGE CHARLES CANTINE

Judge Cantine would go on to be reelected as Ulster County judge in 1910. His death, however, would come two short years later, in 1912. In addition to a career that included serving as Ulster County district attorney as well as county judge, it is possible that Cantine served as trustee or member of more organizations than anyone else in Ulster County history. Those organizations included: New York Historical Association, Kingston City Library, Kingston Academy, the Kingston Club (vice-president), the University and Manhattan Clubs of New York (member), Saugerties Club, Winnisook Club, Rondout Club, Twaalfskill Club, Ulster County Bar Association, State Charities Aid Association, Holland Society of New York, Sons of the American Revolution, Huguenot Society of America, Rondout Lodge No. 343, Free and Accepted Masons and the First Reformed Dutch Church of Kingston.

An account of his life published in the *Proceedings of the New York Historical Association, Volume 11,* concludes that Cantine's funeral, held at the Old Dutch Church in Kingston on July 16, 1912, "was the most largely attended of any man who ever lived in Ulster County." Judge Cantine is buried in Kingston's Montrepose Cemetery.

Dr. Mortimer Downer

In addition to his more than a quarter of a century caring for his Woodstock patients, Dr. Downer also continued his service to improving the Woodstock community. Part of that service included his leadership of the Woodstock Club, which, along with such members as Ralph Whitehead, Louise Lindin, Henry Pepper and others, worked to bring a library to the citizens of Woodstock. When the influenza epidemic swept through Woodstock in 1918, it was Downer, along with Maverick founder Hervey White serving as his nurse, who single-handedly attempted to contain the spread of the illness throughout the town. On Downer's death in 1928, it was reported by the *Freeman* that the gathering of those who attended his funeral was the "largest turnout ever witnessed in Woodstock." Dr. Downer is buried in the Woodstock Cemetery.

The Conines and Emma Smith

No record exists that can shed light on what happened to the remaining Conine brothers, Arthur and Albert. We do know, however, that Emma Smith's road through life following her separation from the Conine family did not go well. According to a report in the *Saugerties Post*, as quoted in the *Kingston Daily Freeman*, Smith had applied to the Saugerties overseer of the poor for admittance to the county home in New Paltz. The report stated that she was "in a pitiable condition, seriously ill" at a home near the Saugerties/Woodstock line. Having not lived in Saugerties for more than a year, as required by law, however, no action could be taken on her behalf.

Everett Roosa

Though he would eventually find his way into the official ranks of law enforcement, Everett Roosa's future as the next Sherlock Holmes would not turn out as he might have hoped. One month after Van Gaasbeek was acquitted, the best Roosa would do to advance his career in criminal justice was to secure a position as a temporary patrolman at the newly constructed Ashokan Reservoir for seventy-five dollars a month. Later, he would advance to the position of sergeant for the reservoir's board of water supply. He would eventually return to Kingston and take on the position of deputy sheriff.

Charles Wolven

Charles Wolven would continue as assistant superintendent for the Kingston reservoirs system. Only a month after the jury's verdict set Van Gaasbeek free, however, extremely high winds swept through the Woodstock valley, causing a great deal of destruction. During the freak storm, a roof on the barn at Reservoir 2 blew off, pinning and injuring Wolven's three children. Sarah Wolven, who had spotted Van Gaasbeek walking along the road to Woodstock on the day Harrison's body was found, suffered, along with her brother, severe bruises on their heads and sides. Another son broke his arm as a result of the accident.

Wolven himself died tragically when, on October 15, 1920, he was struck and killed by an automobile. Charles Wolven is buried in the Zena Cemetery. His wife, Carrie, would live another twenty-five years.

John Harrison

The faithful service of John Harrison for the Kingston Water Department would be rewarded in June 1909 with his elevation to superintendent of the department. He would continue to represent Kingston for a number of years. A mainstay in the Woodstock Methodist Church, Harrison and his wife, Sarah, though they carried the loss of their son Oscar with them, were blessed with two children as well as a number of grandchildren and great-grandchildren. John Harrison died in 1941. His wife predeceased him in 1929. They are buried in the Woodstock Cemetery.

Augustus H. Van Buren

In a strange twist of fate, shortly after the Van Gaasbeek trial ended, Van Buren engaged once again with Cunningham in yet another murder trial. This time, Cunningham reversed the outcome and prevailed in gaining the conviction of Henry Craft for second-degree murder. Van Buren would, once again, appeal. The fortune that was Van Gaasbeek's on appeal, however, would not be the same for Craft. Originally sentenced to twenty years to life to be served at Dannemora Prison, Craft's sentence was eventually commuted to five years.

While Van Buren continued as a prominent lawyer in Ulster County, he, too, would be elevated to the bench. On February 5, 1926, Kingston mayor Morris Block appointed him to serve as special city judge.

A longtime supporter of William Jennings Bryant's aspirations to be president, Van Buren, once again, supported him in 1912. At the time, because of his continued support, it was rumored that with a Bryant victory Van Buren would be in line for a patronage position with the new administration. History tells us that Cornell Van Gaasbeek's defender remained in Ulster County following the election

On September 14, 1911, Augustus Van Buren returned to the history he loved with an address to New York State Historical Society titled *Wiltwyck Under the Dutch*. He would, throughout the remainder of his life, remain a trusted source, writer and lecturer on area history, including a series of articles for the *Kingston Daily Freeman* on life in Kingston following the Civil War.

Augustus Van Buren died on March 1, 1930, at the age of seventy-three. He is buried in Kingston's Wiltwyck Cemetery

Cornell "Corney" Van Gaasbeek

When Cornell Van Gaasbeek died on Monday February 22, 1915, notice of his death received front-page attention in the *Kingston Daily Freeman* the following day. While his two trials and his appeal were the main focus of the story, it was noted that Van Gaasbeek, once freed, never spoke of his ordeal again.

Van Gaasbeek, following his acquittal, did not return to Woodstock, choosing, rather, to live in Kingston. In the years that followed, while he worked a series of odd jobs for a period of time, he eventually found steady employment as a cook for a farm in Gardiner, New York. The farm was called Shawangunk Hall Farm. The farm was owned by Augustus H. Van Buren.

IN THE END, NO one would ever know exactly how Oscar Harrison died or who may have killed him. There would be no further investigations, no further arrests. Almost three years had been spent attempting to prove that the man who fled out of fear on the morning of December 5, 1905, was guilty, though no direct evidence was ever produced that Cornell Van Gaasbeek had struck Oscar Harrison with a hammer on that cold night and left him on the floor of his house to die. Had either George or Hiram Conine lived, it is possible, as Van Buren had suspected, that authorities at the time would have turned their attention to one of them. And yet, if there ever was a confession by either of the Conines, as had been rumored, it went to their grave, just as the parents of Oscar Harrison would go to their own graves without ever knowing who killed their son.

In New York State legal annals, however, some good may be drawn from Van Gaasbeek's long ordeal and Van Buren's defense of his client. Due to the appeal Van Buren had filed following his client's conviction at the first trial, "character and reputation," as the *Freeman* noted, was "established for the first time" by the court of appeals as permissible evidence and would "govern such testimony in future trials in New York State."

Looking back over a century in which the issues of race and criminal justice have remained central to the American experience, one is left to consider how far we have traveled since the Van Gaasbeek trial. In a digital age in which everyone, essentially, can have their opinions and judgments placed before the world, we find, far too often, that individuals remain quick to point to those who are perceived as "different" and, therefore, must be held responsible for something. In short, our quickness to judge others seems to not have advanced too far from when the world readily judged the guilt of Cornell Van Gaasbeek in 1905. To that end, the words of Augustus Van Buren can still speak to us across the decades. In a speech delivered on Sunday, December 8, 1924, to the Kingston Elks Club and reported in the *Kingston Daily Freeman*, Van Buren offered his thoughts on judging others and the hidden stories we all carry within:

> *To judge correctly, you must know not only what he does or does not do, you must know the reason why. I have known more than one man to be cursed or*

damned, the finger of scorn to be pointed at him for something he had or had not done. If we had known the why, our judgment would have been very different. But men cannot wear their hearts on their sleeves. They cannot tell the why. The must suffer in silence. O, the why! The eternal why.

My friends, before you judge, before you condemn, know the why. Do that and the world will be a much better place to live in.

While the world would change little as a result of what occurred in Woodstock in 1905 and, over the next few years, in a courtroom in Kingston, New York, Van Buren's admonishment can still be heeded. While most of us resort to conjecture based on overall patterns of surface evidence, Van Buren's words and Cornell Van Gaasbeek's case serve as reminders that all may not be as it appears.

At its core, in 1905, Van Gaasbeek's case centered on the tragic death of a young white man and his alleged killer. Representationally, despite more than a century of separation, it is also a case that continues to raise questions on how we as a people—as well as the criminal justice and political systems that represent us—work to arrive at just conclusions.

Our local history is full of such examples; examples that, though they might appear as footnotes to a larger story, offer the opportunity more fully to explore who we are as a community. Too often, it seems, we approach local history in an effort to connect family to community or to establish a sequential series of events that we declare as the foundation on which our present rests. And yet, within that history, are the hidden and forgotten stories analogous to the life narratives of individuals like Cornell Van Gaasbeek and Augustus Van Buren. To take up the exploration of such seemingly "smaller" narratives can represent a different way of viewing our history and, in the process, reveal a more honest way day-to-day life actually unfolded beneath that which we represent as our "official" history.

Would that we could be as perfect as some often claim our history to be. History is not nostalgia; it is not necessarily there to make us feel good—though good can certainly be found. Rather, it is the all-encompassing chronicle of interconnecting lives that have formed the true foundation of our communities. Within that history—and equal to its importance—are the everyday lives of the underprivileged as well as those who earn their living by their hands and physical labor; those who give their time without expectation of recognition, those who suffer through and manage an individual or family crisis; and those whose moral compass simply guides them through their day because that is what they expect of themselves and others. In exploring their lives, in drawing from their experiences, we better understand the commonality of the human experience over time. And, equally important, we may find a blueprint on how to better negotiate both the present and the future.

AFTERWORD
THE ROAD WE HAVE TRAVELED

Beneath the surface of our local history in the rural north lies the seldom-discussed issue of race. From slavery to the present day, it has been an issue that all know is present but few wish to bring to the fore. Failure to do so, however, undermines the record we claim to put forward as "our history." It is analogous to a story that is missing an important element of its narrative. In short, while Woodstock can rightfully stand as a symbol of imagination that has, over the years, fostered the spirit of creativity and individualism, its history is not without the same prejudices that have infected towns both large and small throughout New York and the nation.

Often missed in the story that is Woodstock history, a story that relies heavily on early industries and features multiple chapters on the evolution of an art colony, is the essential fact that Woodstock once knew slavery and, for example, that its wealthier citizens were slave owners.

In 1858, Abraham Lincoln offered, "As I would not be a slave, so I would not be a master." Early in the nineteenth century, multiple Woodstockers contradicted those sentiments. John Wigram, for example, who served several terms as Woodstock's supervisor in the early 1800s, was a rent collector for Robert Livingston and was responsible for Woodstock's first post office, was a master, farming his extensive holdings along what is now Rock City Road with three slaves by his side.

Andrew Riselar and Wilhelmus Rowe were also masters. On January 16, 1800, a child named Pine was born to one of Riselar's slaves. As required by a 1799 state law, Risely registered the child with the Town of Woodstock.

Afterword

Prior to his death in 1803, Wilhelmus Rowe, one-time Woodstock judge, Woodstock supervisor and landowner in Zena, prepared his will. Among the "possessions" listed in his will were two slaves: Pompey, valued at eighty pounds, and Elizabeth, "a Negro wench," valued at forty pounds.

In 1790, three years after Woodstock became a town, New York State counted 21,324 slaves among its total population of 340,120. In that same year, 10 percent (2,906) of Ulster County's population could be found in the census column marked "slaves." Within that same census, the first in the new nation's history, the slave column for Woodstock tallied 15 slaves within the township. In 1800, that number rose to 26. In 1810, it was 19.

It would be another seven years, in 1817, before New York State would begin to take steps toward emancipation, granting eventual freedom to all slaves born before July 4, 1799. Again, however, the operative word was "eventual," as the new law granting said "emancipation" would not become effective for another ten years. So it was, on July 4, 1827, that New York's—and Woodstock's—"peculiar institution" finally began to fade into those pages reserved for New York State's less than honorable past. Still, for many, slavery remained the nasty business it had always been. It was not unheard of, for example, for some freed slaves to be kidnapped and secreted to the South to be sold. Some New York slave owners, not wishing to lose out on their "investment," took their own slaves south in advance of the 1827 emancipation date and resold them in states where America's original sin continued to thrive.

Meanwhile, with the arrival of emancipation, Woodstock slaves found themselves with few options. For the most part, it is believed that many stayed on with their former owners working as laborers. Alf Evers, for example, notes that a former slave named "Tom," who had belonged to John Wigram, did not wander far from Rock City Road, where he could be found, in addition to his work for Wigram, selling refreshments to those who might pass by. Other former slaves in Woodstock, unable to sustain themselves economically, found themselves under the auspices of the town's Overseers of the Poor, an early form of welfare in which the town would pay an individual promising to provide for the former slave or indigent person in exchange for work performed on the provider's property or in their household. As you can imagine, it was a system not too far removed from where the former slaves had been. In one such Woodstock case, a young former slave girl named Gin was bound out to Michael Smith, who, in return for providing her shelter, food and "every day clothes," could expect that his charge would faithfully serve him "on all lawful business according to her power wit and ability." And while most providers went about their obligation honorably, it was also a system that saw abuse. An illustration of the potential for such abuse was exemplified in one case in which the town was forced to dissolve an arrangement between a farmer and a young girl when it was found that the farmer "misused and evil treated her and corrupted the Morals, destroyed the virtue and injured the character of sd apprentice." Following the incident, the farmer fled Woodstock.

For most blacks in Woodstock, in the years that followed the Civil War, theirs was a life not dissimilar from the aforementioned Tom or even that of Cornell Van Gaasbeek. What jobs there were usually consisted of those requiring manual labor, subservient to white employers. Perhaps the greatest concentrations of employees in Woodstock were those once hired by the Overlook Mountain House in the 1870s. The establishment recruited former veterans of the Civil War and students from Pennsylvania's Lincoln University. The hotel's black employees worked primarily as waiters for the hotel's white guests; according to Alf Evers, "each guest's waiter courteously helped him make his choice and served him individually." The same group of waiters is also noted in the *Kingston Daily Freeman*'s coverage of President Ulysses Grant's visit to the mountain house in 1873. Following a dinner honoring the hero of Appomattox, press reports note that "the servants of the house, who are our own colored men and brothers, and most of whom wore dusty frocks of blue during our late unpleasantness [the Civil War] are on the back veranda serenading His Excellency by singing army songs." The following day, as Grant left Woodstock, he passed the Woodstock Cemetery, where a number of soldiers who had followed his command were buried. It was also a cemetery where the burial of blacks had been prohibited.

Small-town history, though unique in its own context, seldom wanders too far from our national story. Such was the case in the years following Van Gaasbeek's trial as the Ku Klux Klan, in the early 1920s, found willing support among some residents of Woodstock. Local history notes that on the night of August 21, 1924, Woodstockers were witnesses to a cross-burning on a field just outside of town heading toward the Bearsville corridor. Only a month later, in the very first edition of Woodstock's first newspaper, the *Woodstock Weekly*, local readers were greeted with the headline "Ku Klux Klan Gains More Members." The brief article offered that the Klan had "held several public meetings in Woodstock and added new members to its organization." According to Evers, the efforts of the Klan locally would include vitriol and contempt directed not only toward blacks but also toward Jews and Catholics. Evers further notes that, at the time, local Klan membership was made up of "Woodstock people of right-wing convictions, many business people and descendants of early local families."

As the majority of Woodstockers began to push back against the activities of the Klan and its representations, it seems that 1924 was the high-water mark of publicly displayed racism in Woodstock. And yet, deep-seated animosities toward those perceived as "different" from the long-standing majority do not die easily. Prior to World War II, townspeople, fearing the takeover of local hotels by Jewish owners, worked to limit such opportunities. It was a period, described by Evers, in which "anti-Semitism, long present in Woodstock, now grew and expanded like a weed in a June garden."

Even as late as the 1960s, as young hippies made their way to Woodstock, an unsettled, conservative town reacted openly in a variety of prejudicial ways. As trespassing arrests rose and as benches were removed from the Village Green in an effort to prevent the unwanted visitors from assembling in the center of town, one prominent Woodstocker offered his definition of a hippie. "A hippie," he proclaimed, "is a creature that walks on two legs, full of lice of the head and pubic section, full of communicable diseases, who speaks an illiterate language." Welcome to Woodstock.

It is not uncommon for human memory to want to pass quickly over that which may be unsettling or, at the time, inconvenient to life's narrative. History, however, cannot afford to do so. Woodstock and Ulster County have a remarkable history. It is a history made even more remarkable by the trials and difficulties that, throughout the years, we have attempted to overcome. And yet, in an age when information has begun to overwhelm us, it becomes far too easy to overlook important elements of our past, elements that called on us to examine who we really are as a people and as a community. The story of Cornell Van Gaasbeek is but one such example.

In the long lineage that is our past, Van Gaasbeek's story—and the stories of those lives his trials greatly impacted—may be but a very small piece of a much larger, much more encompassing story. And yet, it is precisely those often-overlooked fundamentals of where we have been that we cannot dismiss. Each story, no matter how small, is a link in a chain that connects us across time. The story of Cornell Van Gaasbeek, the righteous pursuits of Augustus Van Buren, the tragedy suffered by the Harrisons and the context of time and place that surrounded the entire saga opens doors to more fully understanding the road we have traveled. Great events, along with the formidable figures who have led them, are remembered in large part because of the largesse of the record we have been left. And while that by no means diminishes their relevancy, we must constantly be mindful that there

Afterword

is always more to examine. Whether that examination leads us to exploring our own family's place within the context of an era or to "stumbling" over and pursuing stories such as presented in these pages, it is only through such efforts that equally vital elements of our history can be brought forward.

To truly democratize our history requires each of us to research, explore and pass on the past we engage. To do so will, ultimately, present a history that truly represents all on whose shoulders our present—and future—rests.

—RRH

In Memory of Oscar Harrison

Oscar Harrison's grave in the Zena Cemetery. *Author's collection.*

BIBLIOGRAPHY

Clearwater, Alphonso T., ed. *The History of Ulster County*. Vol. 2. Kingston, NY: W.J. Van Deusen, 1907.
Evers, Alf. *The Catskills, From Wilderness to Woodstock*. Woodstock, NY: Overlook Press, 1982.
———. *Woodstock: History of an American Town*. New York: Overlook Press, 1987.
Heppner, Richard. *Woodstock—Everyday History*. Woodstock, NY: Heppner, 2016.
———, ed. *Woodstock Years: Stories and Reflections on the Birth of an Art Colony*. Woodstock, NY: Historical Society of Woodstock, 2003.
Lee, Harper. *To Kill a Mockingbird*. New York: Harper Perennial Classics, 2006.
McManus, Edgar J. *A History of Negro Slavery in New York*. Syracuse, NY: Syracuse University Press, 2001.
New York Correction History Society. "Clinton." Accessed December 12, 2018. http://www.correctionhistory.org.
People v. Van Gaasbeek. Reports of Cases Heard and Determined in the Appellate Division by the Supreme Court Volume of the State of New York, vol. 118, 1907.
Proceedings of the New York Historical Society. Vol. 11. New York State Historical Association, 1912.
Schenkman, A.J., and Werlau Elizabeth. *Murder & Mayhem in Ulster County*. Charleston, SC: Arcadia Publishing, 2013.

BIBLIOGRAPHY

Sylvestor, Nathaniel B. *History of Ulster County, New York*. Philadelphia: Everts & Peck, 1880.

Van Buren, Augustus H. *A History of the Ulster County Under the Dominion of the Dutch*. Astoria, NY: J.C. & A.L. Fawcett, 1989.

Zinn, Howard, *A People's History of the United States*. New York: Harper Collins, 2003.

ABOUT THE AUTHOR

Richard Heppner is the town historian for Woodstock, New York. He is the author of *Remembering Woodstock*, *Women of the Catskills*, **Legendary Locals of Woodstock** and *Woodstock—Everyday History*.

Visit us at
www.historypress.com

www.ingramcontent.com/pod-product-compliance
Lightning Source LLC
Chambersburg PA
CBHW040253170426
43191CB00019B/2398